SPIN-Farming® Basics

How to Grow Commercially on Under an Acre

By Wally Satzewich and Roxanne Christensen

www.spinfarming.com

Step-by-step learning guides to the sub-acre production system that makes it possible to gross $50,000+ from a half-acre.

ISBN: 978-0-615-38409-2

What this book provides: how-to sub-acre farming information.
What this book does NOT provide: legal, accounting or professional business advice or services.

For information on licensing, foreign or domestic rights, or bulk copy orders for educational use, contact Roxanne Christensen at rchristensen@infocommercegroup.com, or at 610-505-9189.

MEET YOUR NEW BUSINESS PARTNER...

You can't reason with her. You can't control her. She does not even have a vested interest in whether or not you exist. She's Nature, and you're going to be working closely with her from now on.

Farming is a nurturing process governed by agricultural practices, but it is also a business driven by economic goals. This tension makes it such an interesting profession. Nature works in slow time, involving overlapping cycles of activity that often take years and sometimes decades to discern. Profit and loss statements are churned out in fast time, month after month.

While most farming systems focus primarily if not exclusively on agricultural practices, SPIN emphasizes the business aspects and provides a financial and management framework for having the business drive the agriculture, rather than the other way around. Contained in these seven SPIN guides is everything you'd expect from a good franchise: a business concept, marketing advice, financial benchmarks and a detailed day-to-day workflow. In standardizing the system and creating a reproducible process, SPIN really isn't any different from McDonald's. Think of it as a franchise-ready farming system that can also accommodate the creative and place-based nature of farming. It is up to you to apply the system based on your own markets, climate and preferences.

In the pages ahead you will discover that SPIN-Farming is sub-acre in scale and entrepreneurial in spirit. It requires minimal infrastructure, so it's easy on the pocket book. It is organic-based, so it's easy on the environment. It fits whatever life style you have, or wherever you are in your life cycle. It can be practiced in the middle of the urban jungle, or on the suburban fringe or on a larger acreage in the country. Wherever you find yourself, SPIN provides a low-risk way to get started in farming and increases your chances of success.

What does SPIN stand for?
S-mall P-lot IN-tensive. But it also stands for the kind of farming that anyone can understand and that more and more are embracing. Like these folks >>>

MEET SOME OF YOUR COLLABORATORS...

Here are a few members of the growing corps of farming visionaries who are using SPIN to get both farms and farming projects off and in the ground.

"The SPIN system has given a lot of young people the opportunity to return to their roots....or start a whole new career in agriculture! Speaking for myself I can say that SPIN has given us the opportunity to continue doing what we love...being stewards of the land...We had hit a wall with traditional agriculture, but now we have found our way again through SPIN!"
Tim Schultz, The Green Ranch, Osage, SK

"I'm creating an urban farm network that's neighborhood-based and makes fresh, healthy food accessible to everyone. One of the primary goals is to bring back the job description of "farmer" and recreate it as a profession for city dwellers. As a non-profit, Urban Patchwork can create programs that pay and teach interns who then go and run their own urban farms throughout the city. It's structured so that the parent non-profit organization supports and reduces costs for the individual neighborhood farms so they can hire farmers and pay a living wage. That will add 50-100 farmers to Austin's demographic!

"SPIN was a wonderful find because I was in the middle of "inventing" the same such concept and set of materials. It was a neighbor and now fellow SPINner who introduced me to it (thanks to Michael!) and it shaved at least six months off my farm development and formation."
Paige Hill, Urban Patchwork Neighborhood Farms, Austin, TX

"I've been reviewing tons of how-to materials that might have even a remote relevance to my sustainable commercial urban farms incubator (SCUFI) program. Whoa, have I waded through vast tonnage of imprecise and generalist chaff looking for kernels of wheat. But not a problem with the SPIN guides. They have virtually zero chaff. Using the SPIN guides as solid intros for people with little or no familiarity with commercial urban organic farming as a business, I just don't know anything better."
James Kalin, CEO, Virtually Green, San Francisco, CA

Still more farming visionaries >>>

MEET SOME OF YOUR COLLABORATORS...

"I just had 20 yards of organic compost dumped on my driveway this morning – there is no going back now!:) Thank you for developing such a user-friendly method for people -it is so much easier to get started this way! I also work for county government in workforce and economic development; I can see how these methods could help to address critical community-wide issues such as local jobs, entrepreneurship, food security, poverty, environmental issues, etc. Food security is going to become an ever larger issue and you have created a very accessible way for people to get in the game in a way that greatly increases their chance of success. Thanks very much for your work; it might just change the world one garden a time."
Geniphyr Ponce-Pore, Program Manager, Business and Enterprise, Larimer County Work Force Center, Fort Collins, CO

"I just started my business here in Waukegan, IL. My business is Waste-Not Gardens, Inc. I am helping my city establish a local food system using the SPIN method. I also am proposing to the city that I will be utilizing a raised-bed, zero till or minimal till method (lasagna gardening). My business is a zero-waste concept. They are very interested and I am moving forward. I am currently communicating with the zoning director as they are willing to make exceptions to the zoning ordinances to accommodate the small scale production. They understand the importance of establishing a sustainable, local food system. I am hoping to accomplish many things with my operation. I can't thank you enough for the development of the SPIN-Farming method!"
Suzanne Abrudeanu, Waste-Not Gardens, Inc., Waukegan, IL

"The best thing I have to say about SPIN was that it gave me a whole new way of thinking about farming. That is, farming with an eye to real income without needing the investment of large numbers of acres and huge debt. As a long time grower for my family and friends, I never thought I was "big" enough to be a farmer. SPIN was my "aha!" moment."
Barb McKillip, Mountain View Meadow Farm, Elbert, CO

"Your guides are excellent!!!! This should really help out our local initiative."
Bill Gardiner, District Conservationist, USDA-NRCS, Salida, CO

"This is our third year SPIN-Farming and we do this as a part-time operation. We would love to expand, as we have more market opportunity than we have time to grow for. We are considering looking for a partner for next season as we have opportunity in new markets and also have had requests to start a CSA. At present, we rely on community garden plots as our primary land base.

Anyway, I love the SPIN guides. They've been incredibly helpful. For me, my take away from the guides was (1) an approach to growing in a systematic way and (2) a good marketing approach. And we love being involved in our local market. I've enjoyed building up some regular customers and getting to talk about our product."
Chad Butler, Butler Family Farm, Aurora, IL

"This is only my second year with SPINing. I have been using 2x20' SPIN beds (65 total) because it worked best for my space. I would recommend it for you as well, as it would give you more diversity and more rotations. I also think 3400 sq ft would be good for starting out, it is better to start out small and do it well then to do too much and burn out, especially if you are farming part-time. The great thing about selling at a farmers market is you don't have an obligation to bring a certain amount. As a newbie, I assure you that you will have failures and successes, as far as what sells and what grows. I have to say that I am so happy I have started using the SPIN methods, they really work."
Nate Clark, Good Earth Gardens, Harrisonburg, VA

These are just some of the hundreds of SPIN farmers who generously offer advice and inspiration in SPIN's free online support group, which is a collaborative mechanism for self-improvement as well as for contributing enhancements to the system. Once you start implementing SPIN, you're welcome to join in. But first you need to...

SPIN-Farming® Basics

...Get with the system!

No hype. Just SPIN.

More SPIN-Farming® Basics>>>

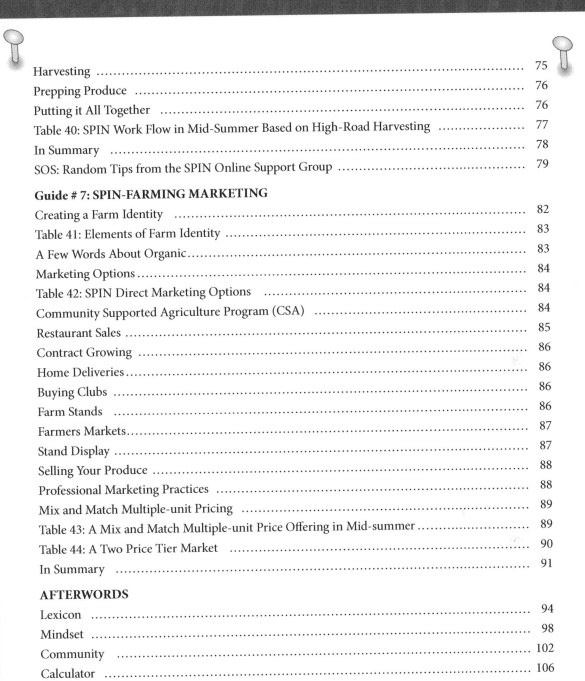

Here is how the SPIN-Farming system works > > >

SPIN *Ideology free* Farming

Think in terms of a production system, not a belief system.

SPIN-Farming® Basics

Guide 1: Overview
What's SPIN-Farming...How SPIN differs from conventional farming...SPIN formulas for success...Harvesting techniques... Marketing...Operating models

Photo courtesy of Dan Bravin, Portland, OR

GUIDE 1: OVERVIEW

SPIN-Farming's Radical New Concept: Sub-acre Commercial Growing

So you want to be a farmer?

You're not alone.

More and more people throughout the world are being called to farming, and they don't fit the usual profile. They don't come from traditional farm families. They don't own much – or any – land. Many do not even live in the country. Some have been educated in other professions, or have had other careers. Some have home or community gardening experience while others have never had dirt under their fingernails. Some want to farm full-time; others part-time.

What unites them all is a curious sense of timing. The amount of available farmland is shrinking. Political systems favor large-scale agriculture. Science is delivering ever more powerful discoveries that take us further and further away from the natural makeup of food.

But in spite of these obstacles, a new breed of farmer is emerging, equipped with two vital assets. The first is market demand. A growing base of customers want a direct connection to the source of their food, and are willing to pay the cost. The second is an ability to approach farming in a radically new way. What they are calling for is a radical new way to farm – and SPIN is it.

What's SPIN-Farming?

SPIN stands for S-mall P-lot IN-tensive. Its organic-based techniques make it possible to generate $50,000 in gross sales from a ½ acre of land growing common vegetables such as carrots, spinach, lettuce, salad mixes, beets, chard, cucumbers, potatoes, beans, radish, scallion, fresh herbs, summer squash and garlic. It requires a modest up front financial investment and can be practiced in either rural or urban areas. A SPIN farm can begin with a plot as small as 1,000 square feet, or it can be located on a 1/2 acre of city-owned land, or it can be multi-sited on several residential backyards.

SPIN-Farming has its own processes and techniques, and they are very different from conventional farming methods, or from home gardening. Here are the defining features that the SPIN learning guides will explain in detail:

- Intensive relay cropping practices
- Balancing production between high-value and low-value crops to produce a steady revenue stream
- Application of organic growing methods, especially the use of locally produced organic fertilizers
- The 1-2-3 bed layout to maximize productivity and revenue
- The 75/25 land allocation rule
- A sophisticated product line that incorporates seasonal crop repertoires
- Highly regimented harvesting techniques

- Direct marketing channels and combination pricing schemes

The SPIN-Farming system is a unique and highly specialized one. If you aspire to be a farmer, you may need to break with what you might have learned as a home gardener. If you are a conventional farmer looking to downsize your operation, you'll need to leave customary multi-acre techniques behind.

How SPIN-Farming Differs from Conventional Farming

Large-scale vegetable farms spanning tens, hundreds or even thousands of acres far outside metropolitan areas require substantial financial investment, rely on mechanized equipment including tractors and tilling and harvesting attachments, require elaborate and expensive irrigation systems, have significant operating overhead and are usually far removed from their markets. In contrast, SPIN farms have modest startup expenses, can be set up in just about any location, rely primarily on hand labor, use existing water sources, have minimal operating overhead and are able to locate close to their markets. Table 1 outlines the differences.

> SPIN farms have modest startup expenses and can be set up in just about any location...

Table 1: SPIN-Farming Versus Conventional Farming

	SPIN Farm	Conventional Farm
Land Base	Sub-acre	Multi-acre
Start-up investment/ overhead	Modest	Substantial
Equipment needs	Rototiller	Tractor
	Hand tools	Tilling and harvesting attachments
	Sink/post-harvesting station	
	Walk-in cooler	
Irrigation	Garden grade hoses and sprinkler attachments	Water lines
		Pumping stations
		Massive piping systems
Utilization of farm resources	Cyclical, closed loop	One way, from depletion to pollution
Off-farm inputs	Minimal	Perpetual
Labor	3-4 workers optimal	Large work crew
Travel time to market	Minimal	Substantial
Markets	Direct access— more control	Removed access— less control

SPIN-Farming has many advantages. And while this system of farming can be adapted by anyone, anywhere, in either rural or urban settings, many of the benefits of SPIN are derived from growing in or near densely populated areas. This runs counter to the predominant way of thinking, but in the first urbanized century, commonly-held assumptions about farming need to be adjusted to accommodate increasing population and diminishing resources.

What makes SPIN-Farming "new and improved" is that it makes it possible to earn a living, or generate a substantial amount of part-time income from a sub-acre land base. Small may or may not be more beautiful, but it is definitely a more efficient and profitable way to farm. Proof of this can be seen in the following SPIN formulas.

The Formulas for SPIN-Farming Success

It has never occurred to anyone to adapt modern, commercial farming methods to a sub-acre land base. Agricultural experts think in terms of tens or even hundreds of acres to define "small-scale" farms. That is why SPIN-Farming is so revolutionary. But to succeed at sub-acre farming requires that you understand and apply precise formulas in order to achieve high income levels.

SPIN-Farming formulas show exactly how you can target $50,000 from a ½ acre, which is about 20,000 square feet. Without understanding these formulas you will probably underachieve on your farm. In fact, most startup small-scale farming operations fail in their first year or two of production, and most conventional farmers do not have a good sense of how to target revenue. So the formulas are one of the most important aspects of the SPIN system.

> SPIN-Farming defines a high-value crop as one that generates $100 per standard size bed.

To understand SPIN-Farming revenue targeting formulas, it's necessary to introduce a few SPIN concepts. One is a "standard size" bed. A bed is simply a small strip of land that is dug up using a rear-tine rototiller. A standard-size bed is one that measures 2 feet wide and 25 feet long, and this is a basic unit of SPIN-Farming .

Next, you need to understand the practice of relay cropping. Quite simply, it is the sequential growing of crops in the same bed throughout the season. Once a crop has been harvested, the bed is immediately replanted to a different crop. Using intensive relay cropping, it is possible to plant and harvest three or more crops per bed, per growing season. Intensive relay cropping allows you to enhance the productivity of your land base several-fold over a conventional farming approach.

To fully understand the formulas, you also need to know what a "high-value" crop is. SPIN-Farming defines a high-value crop as one that generates $100 gross per standard size bed. There are many different kinds of crops that can be grown that will generate $100 per bed. And now here is the connection between all of these concepts. If you can make $100 per crop per bed, and if you practice relay cropping and grow and harvest 3 crops per bed, you will therefore make $300 gross per bed per growing season. So you may be beginning to see how SPIN-Farming can produce much higher revenue than the conventional farming approach.

To make the point even clearer, let's consider the number of standard size beds that can be contained on a sub-acre farm.

Here is how a typical SPIN farm is laid out. Each bed is separated by a narrow walkway, usually no wider than 12 inches. Depending on the size of your farm, you will have a number of series of beds, which will be separated by what is called an exit/access alley. This is a small strip about 2 feet wide, which will be just wide enough for your rototiller. Each series of beds can be accessed with this alley.

To calculate how many beds a given area can hold, the total size of the area is divided by 75, which is the amount of square feet a standard bed occupies, including the walkway: 50 square feet of bed space plus 25 square feet of walkway = 75 square feet. A small allowance also has to be made for the 2 foot access alleys which are especially important when there is more than one series of beds.

As you can see, when you think of a sub-acre in terms of beds, the result is a very precise idea of how much growing space can be utilized, and how that space can be managed to generate predictable and steady revenue. Table 2 summarizes the SPIN farm formulas, and shows how you can use them to target revenue.

Table 2: SPIN Formulas
Each bed is 2 feet wide and 25 feet long

A 1,000 sq. ft. Farm
One series of 13 beds.
13 beds x $300 = $3,900 farm revenue.

A 5,000 sq. ft. Farm (1/8 Acre)
5,000 sq. ft. = Around 60 beds.
5 series of beds with 12 beds in a series.
60 beds x $300 = $18,000 farm revenue

A 10,000 sq. ft. Farm (1/4 Acre)
10,000 sq. ft. = Around 120 beds.
10 series of beds with 12 beds in a series.
120 beds x $300 = $36,000 farm revenue

A 20,000 sq. ft. Farm (1/2 Acre)
20,000 sq. ft. = Around 240 beds.
20 series of beds with 12 beds in a series.
240 beds x $300 = $72,000 farm revenue

A 30,000 sq. ft. Farm (3/4 Acre)
30,000 sq. ft. = Around 360 beds.
30 series of beds with 12 beds in a series.
360 beds x $300 = $108,000 farm revenue

40,000 sq. ft. Farm (1 acre)
40,000 sq. ft. = Around 480 beds.
40 series of beds with 12 beds in a series.
480 beds x $300 = $144,000 farm revenue

The key numbers to remember are the $100 gross per bed per crop, and total bed revenue of $300 gross per growing year.

Now you can see why you should be excited about the revenue potential of sub-acre farming. Using SPIN-Farming methods you can generate high revenue from your sub-acre farm. The key numbers to remember are the $100 gross per bed per crop, and total bed revenue of $300 gross per growing year. If you can achieve those numbers on a large percentage of your beds then you will also achieve a high level of income.

Table 2 illustrates potential revenue if you intensively farmed all of your land. However, a SPIN farm typically will not have all of its land in intensive relay production. That's because good organic growing practices require the cultivation of different kinds of crops to avoid soil depletion, and to break the cycle of pest larvae feeding. Market demand also justifies the cultivation of some low-value crops. Low-value crops are those whose harvested value is considerably less than $100 per standard size bed. These include slower growing crops such as cabbage and potatoes. There are also some types of extended season crops, such as chard and summer squash, which can be harvested and sold for many weeks and which therefore require less intensive production.

So some areas of the farm should be devoted to less intensive forms of production. As you will see in Guide #5, the 1-2-3 farm layout accommodates different intensity levels of production, and the 75/25 land allocation rule is a gauge to determine how much land is assigned to the various types of production. Most beginning farmers don't understand how to allocate land, or don't think in terms of different intensity levels of production. But these are key factors in SPIN-Farming.

…the main benefit of having a walk-in cooler is its impact on your work flow.

SPIN Harvesting Techniques

Another unique concept important to SPIN-Farming is that of "high-road" and "low-road" harvesting. This describes different harvesting and post-harvesting strategies, and they will help determine whether you will be successful as a sub-acre farmer.

High-road harvesting techniques require investing in commercial refrigeration capacity, either a walk-in cooler or upright produce cooler. A walk-in cooler is an insulated room which maintains a temperature of around 35 F to 40 F. The room is cooled with a compressor and fan, similar to an air conditioning unit, except the room is cooled to a much greater degree. Such a room could be located in your garage, or can be a separate unit unto itself. The optimal size for sub-acre farming purposes is around 12 feet by 12 feet. The cost to construct or purchase a walk-in cooler should be under $5,000.

Upright produce coolers measure around 4 feet across, 6 feet high, and 30 inches deep. They operate much like a home refrigerator. They plug in like one, but they have more capacity and are better suited for produce. Costs for used ones vary but should be under $2,000. They can be added on to your operation on a modular basis

Cooling produce after it is harvested removes the field heat, greatly slowing the rate at which your harvested produce degrades. The produce you bring to market therefore has an appealing, fresh appearance, which translates as better quality, which in turn supports premium pricing. But the main benefit of having a commercial cooler is its impact on your work flow. If you have a cooler, you can begin harvesting certain crops early in the week in preparation for your weekly farmer's market, which will be one of your most important direct marketing channels.

For instance, many farmers markets occur on a Saturday. If you have a cooler, you can begin harvesting and preparing some types of produce as early as Monday. The cooler will keep it in good shape until you go to market. By harvesting produce every day during the week, you will be able to harvest and take to market much more produce than if you just confined your efforts to the day before market. And produce harvested throughout the week means you don't have to work overly long hours the day before market.

If you do not invest in a commercial cooler you are relegating yourself to the low-road harvesting approach. Many beginning farmers take this road, without understanding how much better the high-road is. They put themselves in for a very bumpy ride. That's because if you don't have a commercial cooler, you will have to do most of your harvesting and prepping tasks the day before market, and this makes for very stressful harvesting. In fact, the hardship you incur on the low-road may be so great that you might even give up on farming. Most novice farmers are lost over this issue, and many of them might have succeeded if they had invested in a commercial cooler.

> You don't have to quit your day job and risk everything to become a farmer.

SPIN Marketing

Most of your produce will be direct marketed. This means that instead of selling your produce to a middle man, you will be selling your own produce directly to the consumer, or end user such as a restaurant or caterer. By selling direct you are able to keep more of your revenue. And, as already mentioned, one of the best ways to sell direct is at a local farmers market. Another important direct marketing channel is Community Supported Agriculture (CSA) programs, and they will be explained in greater detail later in Guide # 7.

To be a successful SPIN farmer you should aim to sell produce on a weekly basis throughout a 20-30 week period, possibly more, depending on your location. Table 3 provides examples of weekly sales targets you should expect as you progress throughout your farming career.

Table 3: SPIN Weekly Sales Targets
Level 1 Novice farmers (Years 1-3) $500/week for 20 to 30 marketing weeks
Level 2 Apprentice farmers (Years 4-5) $1,000/week for 20-30 marketing weeks
Level 3 Advanced farmers (Years 6-10) $2,000/week for 20-30 marketing weeks
Level 4 Expert farmers (Years 10 and beyond) $2,000+/week for 20-30 marketing weeks

This learning guide series will give you all the background and information you need to start achieving Level 1 sales very quickly in your career. In fact, by using SPIN farm methods, it is possible to bypass the novice stage altogether or enter the apprentice period very quickly.

SPIN Farm Operating Models

SPIN-Farming can fit into many different lifestyles or life cycles. You don't have to quit your day job and risk everything to become a farmer. Or if you are already retired from one career, you can ease into your second career as a farmer. You can operate a viable part-time farm and be content to grow vegetables on 5,000 square feet. This type of farm can easily be located in a city or town, in your own backyard or in a rented garden plot. If you have a partner, you can consider working a 1/4 acre. After you become experienced with SPIN you can move on to becoming a full-time farmer by expanding your production to 1/2 acre or more. Table 4 shows the different scales of SPIN farm operations that can be established.

Table 4: SPIN Farm Operation Models
Part-time very small hobby farm model: One person   1,000 - 5,000 sq. ft. $3,900 - $18,000 potential gross revenue
Part-time large hobby farm model: Two people   5,000 - 10,000 sq. ft. $18,000 - $36,000 potential gross revenue
Full-time moderate farm model: Two people   10,000 - 20,000 sq. ft. $36,000 - $72,000 potential gross revenue
Full-time large farm model: Family   20,000- 40,000 sq. ft. $72,000 - $144,000 potential gross revenue

The case for becoming a SPIN farmer is hopefully by now a compelling one. In Guide # 2 it becomes even stronger because there you will find out how to begin putting SPIN into practice. You will be surprised and encouraged by how easy it is to get started.

SPIN FARMING®

Frequently Asked Questions

Here are answers to the top 3 questions we have been asked since we began pioneering sub-acre farming practices in 2001. If what's on your mind is not answered here, you can find additional answers and resources at www.spinfarming.com, where you'll either find your answer or become even more curious.

1. Can the average person do SPIN-Farming?

As near as we can tell, success at SPIN-Farming, or any other kind of farming, is not determined by education level or prior work experience. What you do need is a deep and passionate interest in farming, which involves working outside long hours in all kinds of weather (some have described it as a calling to farm), a genuine talent for growing, a good business sense and a willingness to invest years in learning, training and building a business. If you have all that, SPIN makes it easier and less risky to get started and increases your chances of success.

2. How many hours per week does a SPIN farmer work?

SPIN-Farming is not based on season extension, so most start-up operations span about 8 months. In the SPIN hobby farm model, during peak season, which is mid-summer for most, a farmer will put in 40 - 45 hours each week, spread out over 7 days. During non-peak months, the hours drop to about 30 hours each week, spread out over 7 days.

In a SPIN full-time half-acre farm model, during peak season, a farmer couple will put in 40 - 45 hours each week, spread out over 7 days. They may have occasional outside help. During non-peak months, the hours drop to about 30 hours each week, spread out over 7 days.

In a SPIN full-time 1 acre farm model, during peak season, a farmer couple will put in about 50-60 hours each week, spread out over 7 days. They may have occasional outside help. During non-peak months, the hours drop to about 35 hours each week, spread out over 7 days.

3. Can SPIN-Farming work in (name any place in the world)?

SPIN is not placed-based. It is currently being practiced throughout the U.S., Canada, Australia, the UK, Ireland, the Netherlands, New Zealand and South Africa. Each SPIN farmer adapts the system to his or her climate, markets, talents and available resources. There are two things all SPIN farmers do have in common — markets to support them, and an entrepreneurial spirit. They are creating their farm businesses without major policy changes or government support. They are highly s-mall p-lot in-dependent.

Read on to get s-mall p-lot in-telligent >>>

21

SPIN
Sub-acre
in scale
Farming

Think in terms of feet, not acres.

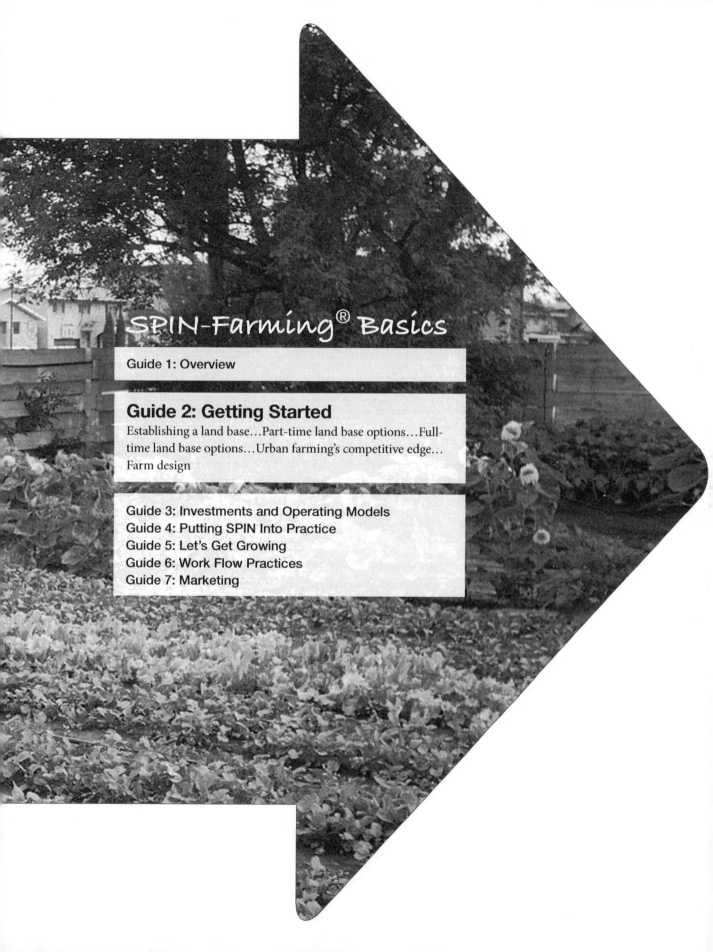

SPIN-Farming® Basics

GUIDE # 2: GETTING STARTED

Establishing a SPIN Farm Land Base

SPIN-Farming provides a range of farming options never before possible because it can be applied in almost any context. Those new to farming usually assume that their only option is to be country-based. But city dwellers do not have to move to the country to farm. SPIN-Farming can be practiced in the middle of an urban jungle, and city growing offers a number of competitive advantages that will be outlined in greater detail at the close of this guide. An inner city farm does not have to be confined to one location, or a single plot. Multiple sites using several plots are also a viable option. For those with access to acreage in the country, a single location is the optimal choice. But if the land is rocky or heavily forested, the farm may need to be assembled on multiple properties.

...city dwellers do not have to move to the country to farm.

City dwellers can generate revenue from a home garden. In this case a few thousand feet of garden space is put into production and farmed on a part-time basis. Single location urban farming can also be done in a very large backyard or adjacent backyard totaling a 1/4 or a 1/2 acre. Another option is corporate-owned or factory land, or city-owned land. Other land base options for urban farms include abandoned land. Every city has different procedures for obtaining access to vacant land, and more and more cities are becoming receptive to re-establishing commercial agriculture activities within their borders. In larger cities, peri-urban areas can be suitable for farming.

Some multi-site urban farms utilize other people's backyards or plots in exchange for produce or cash. Rent for a plot might range from $25 for a very small space and up to $200 for larger-sized areas. People rent their yards to farmers for a number of reasons. Their garden area gets tended and becomes a pleasure to look at. In some cases people are content with getting fresh produce in lieu of a rental fee. Landlords who own a number of properties might also be interested in leasing their properties for farm use since it saves them time, effort and money by not having to maintain the land themselves.

Table 5 summarizes your options when it comes to establishing a land base. As you can see, there are probably more options in terms of locating your farming land base than you thought possible.

Table 5: SPIN Land Base Options		
Rural single-site farm:	Your own land or leased land	
Rural multi-site farm:	Your own land and/or leased land	
Urban single-site farm: Your own backyard	Abandoned land	City-owned land
Factory/Corporate-owned land	Institution-owned land	University-owned land
Urban multi-site farm: Your own backyard	Abandoned land	Leased backyards
Factory/Corporate-owned land	Institution-owned land	University-owned land
Combination of the above		

To determine the best land base option, you first need to know the amount of land you will need, and that is dictated by whether you aim to be a part-time or full-time farmer.

Part-time Land Base Options

A part-time farmer usually targets between $10,000 and $25,000 in revenue, and this requires a 1/8 to 1/4 acre farm, or about 5,000 -10,000 square feet.

If you live on a sizable acreage in the country, it should be easy to assemble a 5,000 -10,000 square foot plot on your property. It could be located near your house and your current water source, and it almost always requires an investment in fencing to protect crops from wildlife.

If you live in an urban area or small town, you might need to use multiple locations to assemble a sizable enough land base to generate this part-time revenue target. A part-time urban farmer may start with their own backyard. They might also arrange to use a friend's yard in exchange for some produce. A next-door neighbor might also be persuaded to lease their small yard for a nominal sum. A few blocks away a relative might offer their yard in exchange for produce. A farmer could also place an ad in a local newspaper and might, for example, obtain two plots within a 10 minute drive, in different neighborhoods. Table 6 shows how you might assemble a multi-site farm in an urban location. Based on the SPIN formula, a 1/8 to 1/4 acre farm in size can generate $500 to $1,000 in revenue per marketing week, during a 20 to 30 marketing period.

Table 6: A 7,500 sq. ft. Multi-site Part-time Hobby Farm	
Your own backyard	1,500 sq. ft.
A friend's backyard	1,000 sq. ft.
Next door neighbor's backyard	500 sq. ft.
Backyard in different neighbor hood	2,000 sq. ft.
A relative's backyard	1,000 sq. ft.
Backyard in different neighbor hood	1,500 sq. ft.
Total	**7,500 sq. ft.**

A part-time urban farmer may start with their own backyard.

Full-time Land Base Options

Since the minimum land base needed to farm full-time is a 1/2 acre to 1 acre, a multi-site full-time farmer may have a greater number of plots to acquire and manage. You might have to obtain up to 20 plots or more, which is easier to do than it might seem. Friends, neighbors, word of mouth, and newspaper ads can all be used in your land search, and the most efficient setup is to have clusters of several adjacent yards in production in any given neighborhood.

Usually you can start out by having a plot where you live, and then you can tap the yards of friends, neighbors and relatives, just as a part-time farmer does. In many cases, you will find that once you begin farming in a certain area, many of the neighbors will like what you are doing, and invite you to expand your farming operation to their backyard.

Other options include a landlord who owns several residential properties with backyards, and who would allow you to farm the land to save on maintenance costs. In many cases, tenants who have outdoor space are not interested in gardening, and they might welcome a farm plot in their backyard. In this case, the rental arrangement can be made either with the tenant or the landlord, but the landlord should be informed of your intentions before you start.

Table 7 shows how a multi-site land base might be assembled for an urban farm around 20,000 square feet in size. The farm is similar in structure to the part-time farm described in Table 6, except it involves a greater number of individual plots. Based on the SPIN formula, a farm 20,000 square feet in size could target revenue in the $50,000 range over the course of 20 to 30 marketing weeks.

Table 7 shows 3 different garden clusters, in 3 different neighborhoods. Clusters of gardens are most optimal. Driving to and fro from plot to plot and from neighborhood to neighborhood costs in both time and money in terms of gas and wear and tear on your vehicle. So the more work you can get done on a given drive to a certain neighborhood the more efficient your multi-site operation will be.

If you want to farm in an urban context there are other options besides the multi-site one. In fact, finding a single site for a full-time farming operation within an urban area may be easier than trying to assemble scattered plots. Institutions such as schools and hospitals or private businesses frequently have sizable portions of unused land which they would consider putting to agricultural use. In some cases you might even find these landowners would contract with you to grow food for their constituencies or employees.

...finding a single site for a full-time farming operation within an urban area may be easier than trying to assemble scattered plots.

Table 7: A 20,000 sq. ft. Multi-site, Full-time Urban Farm	
Garden plot at home	1,500 sq. ft.
Friend's garden plot	1,000 sq. ft.
Neighbor's garden	500 sq. ft.
Neighbor's garden	1,000 sq. ft.
Landlord's garden #1	1,000 sq. ft.
Landlord's garden #2	1,500 sq. ft
Landlord's garden #3	1,500 sq. ft
Plot #1 in Cluster #1	1,500 sq. ft
Plot #2 in Cluster #1	500 sq. ft.
Plot #3 in Cluster #1	1,500 sq. ft.
Plot #1 in Cluster #2	2,000 sq. ft.
Plot #2 in Cluster #2	1,000 sq. ft.
Plot #3 in Cluster #2	1,000 sq. ft.
Plot #1 in Cluster #3	2,000 sq. ft.
Plot #2 in Cluster #3	2,500 sq. ft.
Total	**20,000 sq. ft.**

City-owned property is another option for obtaining single parcels of land. Public officials are realizing that commercial farming is an economically viable strategy for revitalizing neighborhoods and managing vacant land and are beginning to establish formal processes to set up farm businesses in the inner city.

Urban Farming's Competitive Edge

While SPIN-Farming is extremely versatile and can be practiced in either an urban or rural setting, basing your farm operation in or very near a city offers at least 4 competitive advantages over those in non-urban locations.

Water

Water is the first area where urban farmers have it easier than their rural counterparts, because once their SPIN irrigation systems are in place, all they need to do is turn on the faucet. The water used for irrigation and washing is provided by the local public water utility which bears the responsibility of testing, treating and supplying it. Restrictions sometimes do apply, and water service is an ongoing expense, but rates are usually not prohibitive.

...once their SPIN irrigation systems are in place, all they need to do is turn on the faucet.

For rural farmers, the quality and quantity of water is a constant concern. Water in the country frequently comes from wells, and it must therefore be continually monitored for contamination. If it is of poor quality, it cannot be used to wash vegetables. So high-value crops that need to be washed and eaten fresh, such as salad mixes, cannot be grown. Low-volume wells may also limit the available water, and therefore impose restrictions on the amount of watering that can be done and the methods of irrigation used.

Alternative sources of water, such as a stream or river, require a pump site which is expensive to set up and burdensome to maintain. If there are dramatic fluctuations in the water source, the pump site might need to be modified or relocated. So this most vital building block of any farm operation requires much more attention, energy and investment in a non-urban setting.

Wildlife

Urban farmers are free of another hardship that country growers have to contend with – crop damage and destruction caused by wildlife. Salad greens and other high-value crops are difficult to grow consistently in the country because of the constant incursions by deer, rabbits and groundhogs. Farmers have dealt with the problem of despoilment for centuries, and while it can be contained through constant vigilance, the only foolproof way to solve it is to leave it far, far behind.

Climate

Cities are generally recognized as being heat islands, meaning that temperatures there are on average 6-8 degrees hotter than outlying areas. This ironically is due to lack of the cooling effect provided by vegetation. So spring starts earlier, and frosts come later. Winds also tend not to be as strong, since the urban landscape contains built-in wind breaks. As a consequence, urban farmers have a longer growing season because of the warmer micro climate. This in turn allows them to get to market earlier and generate revenue sooner. If you farm in the city you might be the only one selling spring produce during May. And in June you can be first to market with such strong selling items as spinach, scallion, and radish.

Proximity to Markets

Farming in an urban setting provides convenient access to a large and diversified customer base with a wide variety of needs, tastes and spending power, as well as the professional market of restaurants, caterers, institutions and specialty retail shops. Farmers markets, community supported agriculture programs, home delivery services and buyers clubs all provide direct marketing channels that are far less lucrative or even logistically impossible in less densely populated areas. Inexpensive web-based ordering and communication further enhances urban marketing opportunities.

In addition to benefiting from a shorter travel distance to customers and concentration of markets, city-based farmers can also "top-up" their sold out products by quickly returning to the farm, harvesting a second supply, and returning to market before it closes, generating an additional several hundred dollars in sales.

SPIN Farm Design

A farm on a sub-acre land mass needs to be conceived much differently than a home garden or conventional farm. (You will be reminded of this often throughout these guides). A SPIN farm is based on a very specific design.

Home gardeners, and conventional farmers, don't realize there are at least two basic ways to lay out a farm. Many multi-acre farms use what is called the row/walkway design, whereby each row of crop is separated by a space. This space, called the walkway, accommodates a tractor tire, or foot traffic. Multiply this space across an entire field, and you can see that it becomes a highly inefficient use of land, and results in the loss of significant production capacity. For certain crops, such as potatoes, a SPIN farm will still rely on this conventional cropping layout, whereby individual rows of crop are separated by spaces that can be used for pedestrian and working purposes, but the SPIN farm relies mainly on the bed/walkway system.

The bed/walkway design maximizes productivity on a limited land base. A bed is simply a small section of a site, and it is separated from other beds by a narrow walkway. Beds are usually made with a rear tine rototiller, but they can also be made with hand tools if the farm is very small. There is usually no special attempt to raise the beds or make them curvilinear, or use lumber to outline them, as some other gardening approaches advocate. A rototilled bed is flat and ergonomically structured so that it can easily be worked in an upright position. Beds can be a variety of dimensions, but SPIN-Farming largely relies on what is called a standard size bed. As noted previously, a standard size bed is 2 feet wide and 25 feet long.

A bed 2 feet in width is easy to straddle with the legs, making it easy to hand weed and harvest. Beds wider that 2 feet in width can be difficult to straddle, which results in awkward and inefficient work positions, such as kneeling by a bed. Beds 25 feet long are also easy to plant and quickly harvest of their contents. Also, beds 25 feet in length correspond to the length of many types of garden hoses which can be purchased inexpensively. Each bed is usually planted with 2 to 6 rows of crop. For instance, in a bed 2 feet wide you might plant 6 rows of radish. Or you might plant 3 rows of beets. Or you might plant 2 rows of beans.

Also, since SPIN-Farming relies on a technique called intensive relay cropping, which will be discussed in detail in Guide # 4, short compact beds are better for relay cropping purposes than beds of greater length.

An important point to remember is that foot traffic occurs only within walkways, and not within the confines of a bed so as not to compact the soil. Walkways are made up of a narrow strip, usually no more than a foot in width. A series of beds that are laid out beside each other are separated by what are called access alleys which allow for the movement of a rototiller, wheelbarrow and garden cart.

A 1/2 acre SPIN farm might have 240 standard size beds. A perimeter area, which might be a couple of feet wide, surrounds the growing space. It can be kept open, or it can be planted to avoid maintenance. Sunflowers make an especially appealing border, attract beneficial insects and provide decoys for squirrels. The seed heads can be used in crafts that are sold at the end of the season, and the stalks can be ground down with a chipper shredder and used as a mulch or compost. Table 8 outlines the various design elements of a SPIN farm.

…short compact beds are better for relay cropping purposes than beds of greater length.

Table 8: Design Elements of a SPIN Farm	
Standard sized beds	2' feet wide 25 feet long
A series of beds	a number of beds side by side
Walkways	12" or less in width
Access alleys	2' in width between series of beds
Perimeter	fencing, or possibly perennial plants, and/or flowers

Now that you have a basic idea of how a SPIN farm takes shape, Guide # 3 will outline the major financial investment that is required. Starting up a SPIN farm is surprisingly inexpensive.

What to Look For in an Urban Farm Site

More and more first generation farmers are seeking cropland amid concrete. Here are some of the site selection criteria you can use to stake out your city-based farm.

Size – a site's total footprint should accommodate walkways and structures such as a commercial cooler, post-harvesting processing station, storage shed, other workspace and parking, in addition to growing space. For 1/2 acre of growing space, a 3/4 to 1 acre size lot is optimal.

Topography/physical conditions – relatively flat terrain is optimal. The site should have good drainage and not be susceptible to flooding. Farming can be done on a slope or even possibly on a hillside but issues of soil and water runoff become considerations under those conditions.

Soil condition – basic soil tests need to determine that the soil is within the range of state agricultural soil averages, or that it can be improved to achieve this range through the use of organic inputs. In the case of brownfields, the SPIN growing techniques and business model can be adapted to container and raised bed growing.

Sunshine – the site should ideally be in full sun, but partial shade locations can be made to work, as long as shading is not excessive for much of the day.

Utility access – the site should have existing water and electric hookups; if not, city policies allowing for these site improvements at a relatively low cost should be encouraged.

Relationship to community and nearby residences – support of neighbors, community associations and elected officials is critical. In addition, if the farm site is adjoined by residences, a buffer between the farm and those residences may be essential to avoid conflicts over noise and other farming activities that could be perceived as disruptive.

Buffer from non-residential uses – in some situations a buffer may be necessary to protect the organic nature of the field in cases where chemicals are applied or emitted by neighboring uses. Large buffering requirements may greatly expand the size of site needed. Guidelines provided by a state's organic association can be used in these circumstances.

30

Relationship to adjacent non-residential uses - certain adjacent activity can also negatively impact farming. Ideally adjacent uses would have minimal nighttime lighting and low traffic volume. If outside interferences do exist, additional open space or other buffer may be necessary.

Vehicle access — adequate access must be available for a van, mini truck, or similar sized vehicle.

Perceived security - given that farmers work mainly outdoors and their products are outdoors, the neighborhood should offer a reasonable sense of safety for both the farmer and the farm.

Site access - nearby public transit access is desirable.

Land acquisition - City policies need to be encouraged to provide for "urban farmsteading" type programs which would provide assistance in land acquisition to farmers and allow them to build equity.

Farming as Interim Use — Many cities are dealing with shrinking populations and an abundance of vacant land. Making some of that land available for commercial farming on an interim basis can make sense.

Site control and term of site availability — Farming is a highly adaptive and dynamic activity and can therefore be considered as an interim use. In these situations, the length of the lease should be made clear, and a compensatory mechanism may be created for rewarding the farmers financially for any rise in land value that can be attributed to their activity. Sites which for varying reasons can never be developed, may be designated as permanent agriculture sites.

Read on to find out about s-mall p-lot in-vestments >>>

31

SPIN
Low capital intensive
Farming

Think in terms of little or no debt.

SPIN-Farming® Basics

Guide 3: Investments and Operating Models

Major investments…Structures…Irrigation equipment…Farm stand display…Tools…Part-time small low-road model…Part-time large high-road model…Full-time moderate-size high-road model…Full-time, large high-road model

GUIDE # 3: SPIN-FARMING INVESTMENTS AND OPERATING MODELS

Guides # 1 and # 2 introduced SPIN-Farming, outlined the options for acquiring a land base, and described a SPIN farm's layout and design. In this guide you will learn exactly what you will need in terms of equipment and investment to set yourself up in your own operation. And you'll see just how accessible agriculture can be, even for those with very modest means.

SPIN can accommodate a wide variety of scales of operation.

Major Investments

Table 9 lists the three major investments that are standard operating equipment for most part-time farmers, and virtually all full-time farmers. You'll see that the expense ranges are quite broad, and that is because SPIN can accommodate a wide variety of scales of operation, from part-time, very small operations to full-time, sizable ones. Each requires different levels of investment. The various SPIN farm operation models will be discussed and illustrated later in this guide.

Table 9: SPIN's Major Investments	
Delivery vehicle	$3,000 to $30,000
Walk-in cooler	$3,000 to $10,000
Rototiller	$500 to $5,000
Total:	**$6,500 to $45,000**

Rototiller

Most home gardeners don't use a rototiller, and if they do, it is most likely an inexpensive front tine unit, which can break down frequently and lasts only a few years. SPIN farmers should buy the best unit they can afford, and it should be a rear tine unit. Since most SPIN farms are single or two-person operations, a good quality rototiller is a necessity because it cuts down the amount of time spent on soil amending, bed preparation, weeding and soil cultivation.

As explained in Guide # 1, SPIN relies on a technique called relay cropping. Once a bed of radish is harvested, it is replanted within a very short period of time to another crop, perhaps carrots. To replant a number of beds using just hand tools takes too much time. Using a rototiller for bed preparation and soil amending enables you to relay a bed in a few minutes. In addition, the rear tine rototiller creates a flat seed bed ideal for the use of a garden seeder. Your rototiller can be regarded as your work horse, helping you to quickly accomplish the more labor-intensive tasks on your farm, thereby saving you time and energy.

The good news is that a top-of-the-line rear tine tiller can be bought for around $5,000 if new, and substantially less if you buy a used one. Conventional farmers who rely on tractors have to spend tens of thousands of dollars, and compared to a tractor, rear tine tillers are easy to operate and inexpensive to maintain. Very little mechanical knowledge is required. BCS and Troy are good suppliers of rototillers appropriate for SPIN-Farming, and their sales offices are located throughout Canada and the US.

Walk-in or Upright Produce Cooler

As explained in Guide # 1, the biggest decision SPIN farmers have to make is whether their harvesting approach will be "high-road" or "low-road." High-road refers to smooth and relatively stress-free harvesting regimes, while low-road refers to more "bumpy" and stressful work schedules. Commercial refrigeration capacity is key to practicing high-road harvesting techniques. A walk-in or upright produce cooler makes for a more efficient and profitable operation. You will be able to command premium prices because your produce will be of better quality when taken to market, and you can harvest produce throughout the week, storing it in your cooler until market day. The extra produce you bring to market by employing a cooler will probably pay for the cooler in the first year.

A walk-in cooler is simply an insulated room that can be built inside of a garage, or it can be free-standing. The air in the cooler is chilled with commercial refrigeration equipment to a range just above freezing to 40 F. Optimal dimensions range in size from 8 feet by 8 feet for smaller operations, to 12 feet by 12 feet for larger operations. Coolers are specialty structures and require the advice of commercial refrigeration professionals on construction and installation. The costs for a cooler ranges from $3,000 to $10,000, depending on how much work you can do yourself and whether the equipment you purchase is new or used.

Upright produce coolers measure around 4 feet across, 6 feet high, and 30 inches deep. They operate much like a home refrigerator. They plug in like one, but they have more capacity and are better suited for produce. Costs for used ones vary but should be around $2,000.

Delivery Vehicle

Costs for a delivery vehicle vary considerably, depending on whether it is used or new. Most SPIN farmers find a 1/2 ton pickup truck is optimal. Mini vans or cargo vans are also suitable. If you intend to operate a part-time, very small farm, the current vehicle you have for your own personal transportation purposes might suffice. Smaller-size operations might consider a 1/4 ton pickup truck or a mini van. These types of vehicles can double as your personal vehicle.

SPIN Structures

Post-harvesting Station

A SPIN farm's most important structure is a post-harvesting station, where vegetables are cleaned and prepared. Ideally it is situated on grass or gravel, so the area does not get muddy. It should be in a shaded area near a high-quality water source, and it should be located near the walk-in cooler. It should measure 10 feet by 12 feet at minimum and should have a roof or at least an umbrella for shade. It can be either permanent or semi-permanent.

A permanent structure can be made from recycled materials. It consists of a large sink basin and counter and shelf space. A table that measures 3 feet by 7 feet positioned near the sink offers adequate work space. Simple rubber or vinyl bins can be used for washing produce. Spray guns and drip trays can also be used. The hose should be a safe drinking hose. Gray water can be dumped onto the lawn or growing area or captured in a below ground tank for future use. Once produce is washed, it is usually allowed to air dry for a short while by hanging it in cloth bags, or

A SPIN farm's most important structure is a post-harvesting station…

pillow cases, or on plastic mesh trays before it is taken to the cooler where it will be chilled and then either bagged or binned.

Zoning restrictions might preclude this setup for urban farmers operating in a residential area. In this case, a semi-permanent wash area can be used. Again, it is best located on a grassy area. Umbrellas can be used for sun screens and simple rubber or vinyl bins can be used for washing produce. Spray guns and drip trays can also be effectively used in this setup. When you are done washing, you can dump the water onto the lawn or into the garden. Debris can be raked into the garden or composted. Once the umbrellas are taken down, you would never know that the area also doubles as a vegetable washing area. You might also use your garage or other outbuilding for such work as bunching onions, and weighing and bagging produce. If you use your garage, all you need to do is set up a few tables. Tables can then be dismantled after your work session, and the floor can be swept clean and mopped.

Since SPIN generally relies on pre-bagged produce, a good quality digital scale is another standard piece of operating equipment. This allows you to precisely measure the contents of each bag, and costs under $200. Some farmers also use the scale at their farm stand to weigh out produce that they sell by the pound.

A SPIN post-harvesting station will require an investment of between $500 to $1,200 depending on the size of operation, and whether it is a permanent or non-permanent one. Most of it can be easily obtained at a hardware store or local garden center. Tables 10 and 11 outline all that you will need. Table 10 shows the expenditure that will be required for setting up a post-harvesting area for a larger-sized sub-acre farm, ranging up to 1 acre in size, sited in either an urban or rural location. Table 11 shows what the expenditure will be for a smaller sub-acre farm, most probably in an urban location on a half-acre or less, and utilizing many different plots. The post-harvesting area in this case could be located at your home, in your backyard lawn area.

Table 10: Permanent Post-harvesting Area	
Post-harvesting station	$500 to $1,200
Grey water recycling	$200
Permanent tables	$100 to $200
Digital scale	$100 to $200
Drip trays	$50 to $100
Rubber wash bins	$50 to $100
Wash basins/sinks	$50 to $100
Plumbing	$50 to $100
Garden hose and attachments	$25 to $50
Cloth bags/pillow cases	$50
Total:	**$1,175 to $2,300**

Table 11: Non-permanent Post-harvesting Area	
A couple of canvas market umbrellas	$100 to $200
Digital scale	$100 to $200
Wash bins	$25 to $50
Drip trays	$25 to $50
Folding tables	$25 to $50
Garden hose and attachments	$20 to $30
Total:	**$295 to $580**

Shed

A farm shed is needed to store your tools, and possibly to store and dry harvested crops such as garlic and onion, which can be hung from the rafters. Such a shed should be at least 8 feet by 8 feet in size for the smallest farms, and substantially larger for bigger operations. Acre-sized farms could use a structure the size of a small garage. The cost for such structures will depend on the size and whether you can assemble and build the structure yourself. Simple framed wood structures range in price from $500 to $4,000, depending on the size and whether you insulate it.

SPIN Farm Irrigation

SPIN farms use the same type of equipment that a home gardener uses, but it is utilized to create an above ground system that stays permanently in place throughout the season. Both drip and overhead irrigation are used. Ordinary garden hoses and strip sprinklers will work for smaller SPIN farms, while larger operations might use smaller diameter piping in conjunction with garden hoses or drip tape. Brass and plastic manifolds are an important part of SPIN irrigation systems. A manifold is used to construct what are called solid set irrigation systems in which hoses are not moved around and instead stay permanently in place. A manifold allows you to connect a number of garden hoses and sprinklers to your garden faucet, with the flow of water being directed by the turning on and off of valving on the manifold. Plastic or brass Y connectors are also important components of SPIN irrigation, and can be purchased cheaply at any hardware store. Y connectors allow you more flexibility in arranging your watering system.

These equipment costs are in marked contrast to conventional large-scale agriculture. Irrigation setups at large farms typically use expensive aluminum or larger diameter PVC mainline piping and larger diameter aluminum piping. This type of equipment can cost tens of thousands of dollars, as opposed to hundreds, or perhaps a few thousand dollars, for sub-acre farms. And this is one of the reasons why SPIN makes agriculture accessible: the start-up costs are much more affordable. Also keep in mind that if you farm in an urban context, you will not have to maintain a pump and pumping site, as the local water authorities will supply water to your home or site. All you need to do is turn on the faucet! Table 12 lists SPIN's various irrigation components.

And this is one of the reasons why sub-acre farming is so accessible: the start-up investments are much more affordable.

Table 12: SPIN Irrigation Equipment	
Brass and plastic manifolds	$20
Sprinklers	$20 each
Wand attachment	$20
Garden hoses	$15 for 50 ft. of hose
Soaker hoses or drip tape	$15 for 50 ft. of hose
Strip sprinklers	$15 for 50 ft. of hose
Hose repair kits	$10
Couplings	$5
Washers	$5
Total:	**$125**

SPIN Farm Stand Display

The modest cost of a stand display allows you to connect directly with the consumer at a fraction of the cost of a retail outlet.

If you plan on selling at farmers markets or onsite at your farm, you will need to invest in a stand display. This requires an investment of well under $1,000, but design and selection should be done very deliberately. There are many style canopies available for under $300. Inexpensive canvass umbrellas can also be used. Plastic baskets can be used, but select ones that compliment your stand, and that display your produce attractively. Baskets should be fairly shallow. Plastic tablecloths can be used, as long as the pattern on them is appropriate for your stand. Different tablecloth patterns can be used throughout the season, to keep your stand looking fresh and dynamic. Good-looking signage can be made with your computer for a minimal cost, or it can be hand-painted in an artistic way. Sloppy looking hand-written signs should not be used. If you are selling produce by the pound, some localities require a professional digital scale which, as noted previously, costs under $200. The modest cost of a stand display allows you to connect directly with the consumer at a fraction of the cost of a retail outlet. Table 13 outlines the components of a farm stand and their costs.

Table 13: SPIN Farm Stand Display	
Signage	$150 to $300
Canopy or umbrellas	$100 to $200
Tables	$100 to $200, or scavenged
Baskets	$170
Tablecloths	$40
Total:	**$560 to $910**

The Tools of SPIN-Farming

SPIN-Farming is based on the notion of accessibility, meaning that it can be practiced by virtually anyone, even those with minimal resources. Large-scale agriculture has become an arena where equipment manufacturers lure farmers into buying expensive, glamorous and often unnecessary pieces of equipment. Sub-acre growers can easily avoid this trap, and thereby spend only a fraction of what a large-scale producer spends.

So with that in mind, remember: A garden hoe is still a garden hoe. But the required SPIN tools go far beyond a hoe. While such a tool is adequate for a variety of tasks, its use is not suitable for between row weeding of intensively planted crops. Finer tools are required for such tasks, such as a narrow stirrup hoe, cultivator and a colinear hoe. For harvesting, garden forks, scissors and knives are all you need. Larger-scale forms of agriculture frequently require investments of thousands, or tens of thousands of dollars, for specialty harvesting and weeding tools that are mounted on a tractor. So here again, sub-acre SPIN farmers are in the enviable position of being able to enter the world of commercial growing with only modest investment.

A garden hoe is still a garden hoe.

The tools listed in Table 14 can be purchased for around $1,000. These tools will be necessary for part-time and full-time farmers alike. Once the investment is made, these tools will last you for many years.

Spades are used for a variety of tasks, and can be used for prepping beds if a rototiller is beyond reach. Soil can be turned over and then raked flat. Stirrup hoes and cultivators of different widths and styles will make weeding fast, easy and (maybe) fun. A garden fork can be used for a variety of harvesting tasks. A chipper/shredder is ideal for grinding up organic material, such as sunflower stalks, dry compost, leaves, branches and raspberry canes. This material can then be used as compost material or mulch. Good quality 5 to 10 HP units appropriate for sub-acre farms can be purchased new for under $500, and it is possible to find used units that are in good shape.

Table 14: SPIN Hand Tools

Tool	Description	Price
Chipper/shredder	Used for grinding up organic materials.	$200
Wheelbarrow or garden cart	Used to move around materials. Can also be used for harvesting.	$200
Garden seeder	There are different ones on the market but SPIN farmers mostly rely on the EarthWay garden seeder.	$100
Wheel hoe	Two wheeled instrument that can be used for weeding, and for marking rows. The EarthWay wheel hoe is a good model.	$100
Spade	Ordinary garden spade. Used for a variety of garden tasks.	$50
Garden fork	Used for harvesting crops such as carrots and potatoes.	$50
Pitch fork	Used for turning over compost piles.	$50
Stirrup-hoe	A specialty hoe shaped like a stirrup and which easily draws through the soil. Comes in a variety of widths, making them ideal for between-row weeding.	$50
Colinear hoe	Another specialty hoe. A thin blade like hoe that draws very easily through the soil, making it another good between-row weeding tool.	$50
Cultivators	These are pronged tools that draw through the soil. Can be used for a variety of weeding tasks. Wider ones are good for walkway weeding.	$50
Broad-hoe	An ordinary garden hoe. Usually not good for between-row weeding, but still good for a variety of weeding tasks. Also good for hilling potatoes.	$50
Rakes	Ordinary garden rakes used for a variety of tasks.	$50
Knives	Ordinary inexpensive sharp knives are good for cutting spinach and lettuce.	$20
Scissors	Used for a variety of prepping and harvesting tasks, such as cutting fresh herbs and prepping scallions.	$10
Total:		**$1,030**

Basic Investments for a Variety of SPIN Farm Models

In this section, you will see the options for starting different scales of operation and the set up and investment each model will require. Table 15 lists the various SPIN Farm Models.

Table 15: SPIN Operation Models	
Part-time small hobby operation	1,000 to 5,000 sq. ft.
Part-time large hobby operation	5,000 to 10,000 sq. ft.
Full-time moderate operation	10,000 to 20,000 sq. ft.
Full-time large operation	20,000 to 40,000 sq. ft.

Part-Time, Small Hobby Low-Road Model

You can ease into SPIN-Farming with a part-time, small low-road operation. You will need minimal irrigation, and you can replace a high end walk-in cooler with a few used home refrigerators, or eliminate the cooling process completely. Since your production will be low volume, you might be able to use your existing vehicle for deliveries. On this basis, a very small low-road farm could be set up for approximately $3,000. Table 16 lists the typical costs for a low-road, part-time operation. Remember, the "low-road" simply means you are not using a commercial cooler in your operation.

Table 16: Start-Up Costs for a Part-time, Small Low-road Hobby Model	
Tools	$1,100
5 hp rototiller, used	$500 to $1,000
Farm stand display and equipment	$350
A few home refrigerators	$200
Post- harvest station	$200
Small garden shed	$200
Irrigation	$125
Bins	$100
Total:	$2,775 to $3,275

Part-Time, Large Hobby High-Road Model

If you want to start out more seriously, you can set up a sizable part-time high-road model. Your first investment will be a walk-in or upright cooler. The cost for a walk-in cooler ranges from $3,000 to $10,000, depending on how much work you can do yourself and whether the equipment you purchase is new or used. Upright coolers can be purchased for less with used ones costing less than $2,000. Installation is much easier since they can be plugged in like a home refrigerator. Any work you do should be in consultation with a licensed commercial refrigeration professional

Your next biggest expense will be a rear tine 5 hp rototiller, which can be purchased used. You could of course spend $5,000 on a high-quality new rototiller, and if you have the money to do so it is a good investment. Used ones can be purchased for $1,000 and under.

If you have a small pick up truck, or a mini van, this vehicle can double as your delivery vehicle. It is possible to even use an SUV or station wagon, depending on the volume of produce you bring to market. You will probably need to spend a few hundred dollars at most for rubber garden hoses and sprinkler attachments, and several hundred dollars more for garden tools. Stand tables will also be a minimal expense. Table 17 lists the typical costs to start up a part-time, high-road operation. This scale of operation requires an investment of from approximately $10,000 to $13,000.

Table 17: Start-up Costs for a Part-Time, Large Hobby High-Road Model	
Walk-in cooler (8 ft. by 8 ft.)	$3,000 to $5,000
Vehicle	$3,000
Rototiller	$1,000 to $2,000
Tools	$1,100
Post-harvest station	$295 - $580
Farm stand display	$560
Farm shed	$500
Irrigation equipment	$200
Bins	$100
Total:	**$9,755 to $13,040**

Full-Time, Moderate-Size High-Road Model

If as a part-time farmer you made an initial investment in a walk-in cooler, and already have a delivery vehicle, your transition to a moderate-size full-time operation will be very easy. If you expand your land base, you might need to trade in your rototiller for a bigger one. A full-time operation will require a 1/2 ton truck or panel van, either of which can be purchased used, for under $10,000 depending on the year and condition. You should purchase as good a quality vehicle as you can afford.

A full-time farmer uses the same seeding and hand tools as a part-time farmer, so there is usually no additional investment required for tools. If you did not purchase a walk-in cooler as a part-time farmer, now is the time. You should not even consider becoming a full-time farmer unless you are prepared to make this investment. The minimal size cooler you should build is one at least 8 feet by 8 feet; building a larger one, around 12 feet by 12 feet, will allow you to expand your operation in the future without having to build a larger cooler.

You will also have to spend more to upgrade irrigation. Unlike large-scale farms, which require tens of thousands of dollars for equipment, a full-time SPIN operation merely requires more garden hoses and valving which can be purchased at your local hardware store or garden center.

As your operation gets larger you will also need more bins, and the cost here should be approximately $200. You might also decide to spend more on your post-harvesting area, by making it a permanent structure with roof, sinks and running water. This scale of operation requires an investment of approximately $16,000 to $25,000. The biggest variable will be the expenditure on a vehicle. If you already own a pickup truck or a van, you will not have this expenditure, so start-up costs can be kept to less than $11,000 for this scale of operation.

> If you did not purchase a walk-in cooler as a part-time farmer, now is the time.

Table 18: Start-up Costs for a Full-Time, Moderate-Size High-Road Model

Vehicle	$5,000 to $10,000
Walk-in cooler (8 ft. by 8 ft)	$3,000 to $5,000
Rototiller	$2,000
Post-harvest station	$2,000
Irrigation	$1,000 to $2,000
Farm shed	$1,000 to $2,000
Tools	$1,100
Farm Stand display and equipment	$560
Bins	$200
Total:	**$15,860 to $24,860**

Full-Time, Large High-Road Model

If you are ready and have the means to set up a large full-time operation, you will invest in a large rototiller, install a large, state-of-the-art walk-in cooler, and buy a new cargo van or pickup truck. Several thousand dollars should be spent on irrigation equipment. A significant upgrade of your farm stand display is also a worthy investment. But as you can see in Table 19, even a large, top-of-the-line SPIN operation requires a fraction of the investment that a conventional multi-acre farm requires. If you spend around $5,000 on your cooler, get a used pickup truck and a used rototiller, your start-up costs are substantially less than if you start out with new equipment. Costs for starting up a full-time high-road farm can vary from approximately $20,000 to $57,000.

Table 19: Start-Up Costs for a Full-Time, Large High-Road Model	
Vehicle	$5,000 to $30,000
Walk-in cooler (12 ft. by 12 ft.)	$5,000 to $10,000
Rototiller	$2,000 to $5,000
Irrigation equipment	$2,000 to $4,000
Farm shed	$2,000 to $4,000
Post-harvest station	$2,000
Tools	$1,100
Farm stand display	$700
Bins	$300
Total:	**$20,100 to $57,100**

SPIN's Bottom Line: Little or No Debt

SPIN farmers, whether part-time or full-time, are in the enviable position of being able to set up their farm businesses for under $20,000, in most cases. There are not many businesses where this is possible. And that's what makes SPIN-Farming so revolutionary and appealing: it makes commercial agriculture accessible to anyone, anywhere. Conventional large-scale farming requires several hundred thousands of dollars and is usually accompanied by a huge debt load. Most SPIN farmers should not have to assume a debt burden, or if they do, it will be a manageable one.

In Guide # 4 you'll find all the know-how you'll need to get you growing.

![SPIN FARMING logo]

Farm Better and Easier with SPIN Favored Suppliers

Over the past four years, SPIN farmers have cultivated a growing network of suppliers for all the gear they need to farm easier and better. Here is who they recommend for the major investments you'll need to make.

Rototillers

BCS-America, www.bcs-america.com, nationwide dealers, USA
Earth Tools BCS, www.earthtoolsbcs.com, 502-484-3988, Owenton, KY USA
Troy-Bilt, www.troybilt.com, nationwide dealers, USA and Canada
Mantis, www.mantis.com, 800-366-6268, Southampton, PA USA

Refrigeration

Coolbot, www.storeitcold.com, 888-871-5723, New Paltz, NY USA
KOOLJET Refrigeration Systems, www.kooljet.com, 866-748-7786,
  Tillsonburg, ON CANADA

Farm Stand Tents/Tarps

Rainbow Country Peddler, www.rainbowcountrypeddler.com, 800-388-8277,
  South Vienna, OH USA
A. Steele Co./EZUp Canopy, www.ezup4less.com, 800-693-3353, Stockholm,
  WI USA

Structures (permanent and non-permanent)

Clearspan, www.clearspan.com/fabric/structures/home, 866-643-1010,
  South Windsor, CT USA
FarmTek, www.farmtek.com/farm/supplies/home, 800-327-6835, Dyersville,
  IA USA

Portable Restroom/Washing Facilities

Sinksnmore, www.sinksnmore.com, 877-977-4657, nationwide dealers

Tools

A.M. Leonard, www.amleo.com, 800-543-9855, Piqua, OH USA
BlueStone, www.bluestonegarden.com, 866-543-1222, Minneapolis, MN USA
  (offers wolf garten tools)
Clean Air Gardening, www.cleanairgardening.com, 888-439-9101, Dallas,
  TX USA
Green-n-Easy, www.green-n-easy.com, Elkhart, IN USA (specializes in
  Earthway products)
Earthway Outlet, www.earthway-outlet.com, 800-251-8824
Garden Harvest Supply Company, www.gardenharvestsupply.com, 888-907-
  4769, Berne, IN USA

Equip yourself with lots more SPIN-favored suppliers of tools and gear
at www.spinfarming.com.

45

SPIN Entrepreneurially driven Farming

Think in terms of farming as a small business in a city or town.

SPIN-Farming® Basics

Guide 4: Putting SPIN Into Practice

Key concepts…Utilizing standard-size beds…High and
low-value crops…Cropping levels of different intensity…
Farm layout…Structured workflow…Market stand pricing…
SPIN's three most important concepts…Putting SPIN-Farming
concepts into play

Photo courtesy of Dan Bravin, Portland, OR

GUIDE # 4: KEY CONCEPTS

Putting SPIN-Farming Into Practice

While it can be adapted by anyone, anywhere, many of the benefits of SPIN are derived from growing in or near densely populated areas.

This guide will introduce the system's key concepts you'll need to understand to start putting SPIN into practice. To understand these concepts, remember that SPIN-Farming introduces a new scale of farming. To help make this clear, one acre equals about 40,000 square feet, so SPIN farmers are giving new meaning to the term "back forty" because they think in terms of feet, not acres. The land base for many SPIN farmers is no bigger than some people's backyards and front lawns and neighborhood lots. In fact, the land base for some SPIN farmers is backyards, front lawns and neighborhood lots. So SPIN integrates vegetable farming into the built environment without conflict. While it can be adapted by anyone, anywhere, many of the benefits of SPIN are derived from growing in or near densely populated areas.

Utilizing Standard Size Beds

The basic unit of SPIN-Farming is a standard size bed, which is one that measures 2 feet wide and 25 feet long. A bed of this proportion is easy to straddle with the legs, allowing for efficient performance of farming tasks, such as planting, weeding, and harvesting. Beds much wider than 2 feet are difficult to straddle, resulting in the need to kneel beside a bed, or to step into a bed, which is something to be avoided because it compacts the soil. Beds are 25 feet long because it is easy to crop the contents of such a bed over the course of one or two marketing weeks, and get the bed replanted quickly to another crop. Beds are made with a rear tine rototiller to save on labor, although it is feasible to make a bed with hand tools under certain conditions.

High and Low-Value Crops

SPIN-Farming relies on the notion of high and low-value crops. A common mistake of many novice sub-acre farmers is to grow too many low-value crops, thereby depressing earnings from their land base. One of the aims of the SPIN method is to produce substantial cash flow as early in the season as possible, and key to that is growing as many high-value crops as possible.

The commonly accepted definition of a high-value crop is one that generates more revenue per acre than a conventional grain crop. SPIN utilizes a much more specific definition, with a high-value crop being one that generates at least $100 per standard size bed per harvest. Obviously the more high-value crops you grow, the more revenue will be produced. But market demand and good growing practices call for the cultivation of lower-value crops as well.

What should be avoided is devoting too much production to low-value crops because it takes too long to begin generating cash flow. Also, it is risky to stake revenue on a limited number of crops since weather or disease problems could significantly reduce production and income. Guide # 5 will provide detailed crop selection and show what type of prices and per bed yields are necessary for a crop to achieve high-value status. Tables 20 and 21 list typical high and low-value crops.

Table 20: Typical High-value Crops
Beets
Carrots
Fresh herbs
Lettuce
A variety of leafy greens
Radish
Scallion from sets
Spinach

Table 21: Typical Lower-value Crops
Green Beans
Cabbage
Corn
Peas
Potatoes
Winter Squash

Cropping Levels of Different Intensity

A SPIN farm is laid out using two different types of relays. Relay cropping simply refers to the sequential growing of crops. The intensive relay area is where 3 or more crops are grown on a sequential basis throughout the season. This is the most dynamic and labor-intensive part of a SPIN farm, where high revenue targets can be achieved. In an intensive relay area, you attempt to relay high-value crops only, such as those listed in Table 20. These crops tend to be quick growing and can be used in what are called 3 member relays. Table 22 shows a few examples. There are many possible combinations of relay cropping sequences, and part of the challenge and fun is to discover what works well for you in your climatic zone. In many cases, SPIN farmers are able to achieve 4 and 5 member relays.

Table 22: Examples of 3 and 4-Member Relays			
Spinach >	Radish >	Carrots >	
Scallion >	Lettuce >	Spinach >	
Lettuce >	Scallion >	Baby dill >	
Radish >	Radish >	Scallion >	Spinach
Lettuce >	Baby dill >	Lettuce >	Radish

Beds in an intensive relay area, once harvested of their contents, are usually replanted within a week. This area can be highly responsive to market demand or weather conditions and can be utilized for ad hoc decisions during the growing season. However, a SPIN farm does not consist entirely of an intensive relay area. Another area used on SPIN farms is called a bi-relay area. This is an area where 2 crops are grown on a sequential basis. High and low-value crops could be grown here. This sort of area allows you to expand your crop repertoire, so you bring to market a wider range of produce items. In this area you might grow crops that take longer to mature and then relay them with a quick growing crop. As you can see, there are many possibilities.

While relay plantings in the intensive relay area are usually done within a week, and often within a day of a crop being harvested, relays in the bi-relay area needn't be as hurried. Sometimes you might wait until a whole section of this area is harvested, over several weeks, before the area is replanted to other crops. Examples of bi-relays are shown in Table 23.

Table 23: Examples of a Bi-relay	
Beans >	Lettuce
Peas >	Carrots
Potatoes >	Beans

A SPIN farm also includes a single crop area. In this area there is no sequential growing of crops. In this you area you might grow tomatoes, winter and summer squash, onion from seed and parsnips.

SPIN Farm Layout

The smaller your SPIN farm the larger the intensive relay area should be. If you have a very small farm, say around 5,000 square feet, you may want to have all of it devoted to intensive relay production. If your farm is closer to an acre, then you might have around 1/4 of your farm in intensive relay production, and the rest of it in bi-relay and single-crop production. The main objective with cropping levels is to allocate different parts of your land to different areas of cropping intensity with the 3 area of your farm being the intensive relay area where 3 or more crops per bed per season are grown; the 2 area of your farm being the bi-relay area where 2 crops per bed per season are grown, and the 1 area of your farm being where only one crop per season is grown.

If you plan on farming several different sites, the SPIN approach is especially helpful in deciding how to strategically farm each one. For instance, you might turn the plot in your own backyard into an intensive relay area, while plots furthest from your home can be utilized for single crops, such as onions or potatoes. If you farm in the country, you might decide to fence off some of your best land and turn it into an intensive relay area, where you grow the highest value crops. Regardless of where you grow, allocating your land base to different areas of cropping intensity is a key consideration, and SPIN guides you towards the most efficient and profitable use of your land base.

The deliberate and disciplined manner used in laying out a SPIN farm also applies to structuring your work flow. During the course of a farming season time must be allocated for planting, weeding, watering and harvesting. If you use a rototiller, the amount of time spent on planting will be minimal compared to more labor intensive tasks of sub-acre growing. Weeding is an ongoing activity and is best accomplished using a systematic approach. Watering needn't be a difficult task, once you have installed your irrigation system.

The most stressful task of any sub-acre farm is harvesting. Most farming schools-of-thought don't distinguish between what amounts to two very different approaches to harvesting, and this in part explains why so many new small-scale farms don't make it past their first year or two of production.

If you plan on farming several different sites, the SPIN approach is especially helpful in deciding how to strategically farm each one.

The two harvesting approaches are differentiated by whether or not a walk-in cooler is part of the operation. A walk-in cooler is a small room or building that you might locate in your garage, or it might be free standing. It chills produce from around 33F to 40F. The room or structure might be around 12 feet by 12 feet, depending on the size of your operation.

As explained previously, if you use a walk-in cooler, SPIN-Farming refers to this as the "high-road" harvesting approach. It simply means you are in for a better and smoother ride. The high-road allows you to harvest produce throughout the week in preparation for your weekly sales, which will most likely include a weekly farmers market. Once produce is harvested and prepped it is stored in the cooler in bins or bags until market day.

Table 24 gives you an idea of what a work flow would look like when you employ the high-road harvesting approach. Enough time is left in each day to allow you to perform your other farming tasks. Harvesting and prepping might be done during cooler parts of the day, such as early morning and evenings, while weeding, which is less challenging, can be done in the afternoon. Using the high-road approach will allow you to structure your work week in a more flexible and efficient manner.

Contrast this with taking the low-road and forgoing the use of a walk-in cooler. Using this approach means having to do your harvesting work much closer to market day. Most of the work will have to be done on Friday, with work often extending late into Friday night. It could also be likely that you would have to get up very early on Saturday morning and do more work, just before market. The produce you harvested on Friday may or may not be in good shape. What is guaranteed is that you will be tired and grumpy at market.

There is much more that can be said about the high and low-road harvesting approaches, but the important point is that a walk-in cooler smoothes out the harvesting work flow so that it is not all concentrated into a single day and allows for much less stressful harvesting. A walk-in cooler will also mean that your produce will be of better quality when brought to market, because most of the field heat will have been removed. This will in part help you obtain better prices. You will also be able to bring to market a greater quantity of produce than if you relied on a day before market harvesting blitz.

> Using the high-road approach will allow you to structure your work week in a more flexible and efficient manner.

Table 24: High-road Harvesting Work Flow

Monday	Scallion work
Tuesday	Carrot work
Wednesday	Bean and potato work
Thursday	Leafy green work
Friday	Odd and ends
Saturday	Day of market

You have to make
good prices happen.

Market Stand Pricing

As you can see, SPIN-Farming is based on well-conceived notions about how to structure your work week. But along with the great deal of attention to farm layout and work flow, just as much attention must be given to how you sell your produce at your market stand. Since you are a sub-acre farmer, you will not be able to sell your produce on a high volume/low price basis, as is the case with larger scales of production. Your approach will be just the opposite.

Since you are a small producer, your volume of production will be relatively low. The only way to make a living from a low level of production is to get high prices. Direct marketing in part makes this possible, but you must go beyond simply bringing your produce to market and hoping for the best price. You have to make good prices happen.

SPIN-Farming relies on mix and match multiple unit pricing. This simply means you pre-bag or bunch your produce into discrete unit sizes, and sell your items at market using one, two, or possibly three different price tiers. Table 25 outlines the multi-unit pricing approach.

Table 25: Two Price Tier Market

These items $1.50 or any 3/$4.00:

  Radish bunches

  Green onion bunches

  Dill bunches

  Garlic bunches (fresh)

These items $3.00 per bag/unit or any 2/$5.00:

  2 lb. bags of new Potatoes

  1 lb. bags of new Carrots

  Beet bunches

  1 lb. bags of Green beans

  1/2 lb. bags of Salad mix

What you will discover is that with this type of pricing technique customers become less price conscious and will be more willing, if not eager, to spend money at your market stand. This pricing strategy will be discussed in more detail in Guide # 7.

Summarizing SPIN'S Three Most Important Concepts

By now you can see that SPIN-Farming takes a radically different approach to farming, from farm layout to how you structure your work week, to how you price your produce. There are still many other different aspects to learn, bit if you can get a handle on the ideas outlined in Table 26, you are well on your way to becoming a successful SPIN farmer.

Table 26: SPIN-FARMING's Three Important Concepts
Farm Layout
Different levels of cropping intensity in different areas of your farm
The smaller your farm the more intensive it must become
High-road harvesting
Walk-in cooler allows for smoother work flow
Walk-in cooler allows you to bring to market more produce, and of better quality
Market Stand Pricing
Mix and match multiple-unit pricing
One, two, or three price tiers

Putting SPIN-Farming Concepts into Play

There is no absolute right or wrong way to put these concepts into play, and there is no single plan that will work consistently. Continual adjustment is needed from season to season, and year to year. This is in stark contrast to conventional farming's approach of "plant it and forget about it". SPIN-Farming is continual trial and error, and it's what makes it infinitely exciting and satisfying.

So let's get growing in Guide # 5.

Think in terms of local inputs that are low-cost or free.

SPIN-Farming® Basics

GUIDE # 5: LET'S GET GROWING

As you now understand, SPIN farms are laid out using areas devoted to different levels of cropping intensity. The 1-2-3 rule divides the farm into three areas which are shown in Table 27. Area 1 is the least intensive, single crop area. Here you grow lower value, long-season crops. Area 2 is the bi-relay area where 2 crops per bed are grown sequentially. Both lower and higher value crops are grown here. Short season crops might be relayed with longer season ones. Area 3 is where intensive relay cropping occurs. This area has the highest earnings potential and is the most labor intensive. Here, you sequence 3 or more high-value crops per bed, per growing season.

Table 27: Different Areas of Cropping Intensity

Area 1 Single crop area

Strategy: 1 crop is grown per season

Crops: Long season crops such as garlic and onion, late season potatoes, shallots, summer and winter squash, and tomatoes

Layout: Plots use conventional row/walkway structure. Rows can be any convenient length. Beds are not used.

Area 2 - Bi-relay area

Strategy: 2 crops per bed per season grown sequentially. Often, short season crops are relayed with longer season crops.

Crops: Beans, beets, carrots, peas, potatoes

Relay sequence: Carrots>Carrots, Spinach>Beans, Peas>Lettuce

Layout: Bed/walkway design. Beds are 2 ft. by 25 ft. long; beds 50 ft. long can also be used.

Area 3 - Intensive relay area

Strategy: 3 or more short season crops per bed per season grown sequentially

Crops: Carrots, fresh herbs, leafy greens, radish, scallion

Relay sequence: Radish>Lettuce>Spinach, Spinach>Carrots>Radish

Layout: Bed/walkway system. Beds are 2 ft, wide and 25 ft. long.

The smaller your farm the larger Area 3, the most intensive growing area, should be. A useful guide is to think in terms of the 75/25 rule: farms smaller than a 1/4 acre should have at least 75% or more of their land base in intensive relay production. Larger farms, 20,000 square feet and larger, can afford to devote more land to bi-relay and single-crop production.

Crops to Consider Growing for Market

A SPIN farmer aims to grow a different choice and wider variety of crops than conventional large-scale growers. For instance, corn and pumpkins are not good sub-acre crops because they tie up a land base for a long period of time and are too low value. SPIN calls for an emphasis on high-value crops, though a portion of the farm is allocated to the production of low-value ones to help maintain soil health, minimize the risks of crop failure, and to have a greater number of items to sell at market. It should be emphasized again that sub-acre farmers cannot afford to grow crops that have low marketability. Crops need to be selected based on what is most popular within a specific market. Experimentation with exotic items can lead to the discovery of a new best-seller, but consumers tend be conservative, so unknown items should be introduced on a limited basis.

> ...sub-acre farmers cannot afford to grow crops that have low marketability.

Table 28 lists typical highly marketable high-value crops. Salad mixes are consistent best sellers. A salad mix can contain many different ingredients, with usually lettuce and cut spinach being the main items. Smaller amounts of other specialties such as radicchio, young chard and beet greens and baby mesclun greens can be added. Salad mixes differ from mesclun mixes in that the ingredients of a salad mix are chosen by the farmer, while mesclun mixes contain the assortment of lettuce and greens offered in commercial seed mixes. Washed and bagged salad or mesclun mixes can be sold for as high as $10.00 to $15.00 per pound.

Scallion is usually very marketable and should therefore always be in production so that it is available throughout the entire growing season. It is easy to grow from what are called onion sets. Bunched onion is similar to scallion, except the onion part is larger and usable as an onion. Carrots, radish, fresh herbs such as dill and basil and green garlic, which is garlic at an early stage of growth, are other popular items.

Leafy greens is a broad category that includes whatever greens are popular in a particular locale, such as beets, chard, collards and kale.

Table 28: Typical High-value Crops
Carrots
Fresh herbs
Green garlic
All leafy greens
Bunching onion
Radish
Salad/mesculun mixes
Scallion

Table 29 lists crops that usually do not achieve high-value status, but are still very marketable, and should thus be grown on some basis. In general, the smaller the farm the less of these crops, but are still very marketable. The larger the sub-acre farm becomes the more of these lower value crops can be put into production.

Table 29: Typical Lower-value Crops
Green beans
Cabbage
Cucumbers
Garlic
Onions
Peas
Peppers
Potatoes
Shallots
Summer squash
Tomatoes

To give you an idea of how to balance the selection between high-value and low-value crops, Table 30 ranks the importance of crops on a moderately-sized SPIN farm in the 1/2 acre, or 20,000 square feet, range. Leafy greens and carrots will be the 2 most dominant crops grown in the largest quantities. Scallion, bunching onion and potatoes will also be grown along with radish and green beans. Many other crops will also be grown and their importance will vary from farm to farm.

Table 30: Relative Importance of Crops for a Typical SPIN farm
Leafy greens
Carrots
Scallion, bunching onion
Potatoes
Green beans
Radish
Other crops

Table 31 lists crops that are consistently strong sellers at market but which are not always available because of low supply. A planting plan that produces a steady supply of these items will allow you to take advantage of low supply conditions, and provide a predictable and steady income.

Table 31: Items Frequently in Short Supply at Market
Carrots, bagged, small to mid-size
Garlic
Radish bunches
Salad mixes
Scallion bunches
Shallots

SPIN Farm Cropping Strategies

This section will discuss specific crops and how you can incorporate them into your farm planting plan. You will also be introduced to another important SPIN-Farming tool: a price/yield combination chart. This will enable you to see what it takes to turn a crop into a high-value one defined as one whose harvested value from a standard size bed, which is 2 feet wide and 25 feet long, is $100.

Leafy Greens

The leafy green category includes a wide range of crops, but the defining characteristic is that the leafy green portion of the vegetable is the most marketable aspect of that item. Beets with tops, chard, lettuce, mesclun mix, salad mix and spinach.

Spinach is a quick-growing green that does well in cooler temperatures, in the spring and fall, and should be one of the first items to be included in a spring line of produce. Salad mixes can include a variety of lettuces, radicchio and any other young greens, such as baby rainbow chard and bulls blood beet leaves.

The SPIN growing approach for leafy greens is called the Week-after-Week leafy green strategy which aims to target 100 to 500 units of leafy green sales per marketing week, depending on the size of your farm. Examples of leafy greens that can be offered throughout the entire season are listed in Table 32.

The SPIN growing approach for leafy greens is called the Week-after-Week leafy green strategy which aims to target 100 to 500 units of leafy green sales per marketing week…

Table 32: Spring, Summer and Fall Offerings of Leafy Greens

Spring
- 100 1/2 lb. bags of spinach
- 100 1/2 lb. bags of cut lettuce
- 100 1/2 lb. bags of mesclun mix

Summer
- 50 bunches of beets
- 50 bunches of chard
- 100 bags of salad mix
- 50 bags of mesclun mix
- 50 bags of head lettuce

Fall
- 50 bags of spinach
- 50 bunches of collards
- 50 bunches of chard
- 100 bags of salad mix
- 50 bags of cut lettuce

Each season, and each week, would see a variation in the types of greens that are available, but the overall aim is to bring to market a consistent weekly supply of leafy greens. Of course more production can be scheduled during times of short supply, such as in early spring when few growers have greens, but a weekly base line of a steady quantity of leafy greens should always be maintained. A weekly target of 300 units priced at $3 per unit retail would produce a predictable weekly income of $900 throughout the season.

Table 33 shows what happens when the high-value concept is applied to leafy greens. Again, a high-value crop is defined as one where the harvested value of a bed 2 feet wide and 25 feet long is $100.

Table 33: Yield/Price Combinations for Leafy Greens

40 units (bags) of greens per standard bed
- a) @$1.00 per unit = $40.00 per bed
- b) @$2.00 per unit = $80.00 per bed
- c) @$3.00 per unit = $120.00 per bed

50 units (bags) of greens per standard bed
- d) @$1.00 per unit = $50.00 per bed
- e) @$2.00 per unit = $100.00 per bed
- f) @$3.00 per unit = $150.00 per bed

60 units (bags) of greens per standard bed
- g) @$1.00 per unit = $60.00 per bed
- h) @$2.00 per unit = $120.00 per bed
- i) @$3.00 per unit = $180.00 per bed

Leafy greens achieve high-value status under a number of different price/yield combinations. You should have no problem getting at minimum $2.00 to $3.00 per unit for your leafy greens. Salad mixes and spinach might be sold in 1/2 pound quantities, while you can experiment with what works for other leafy greens. Novice SPIN farmers can target 100 units of leafy greens per week. Expert SPIN farmers, who know how to get steady production and market effectively, can target 500 or more units per week.

Most types of leafy greens can be planted with an Earthway seeder in 2 foot wide beds, with 2 - 4 rows per bed, depending on the type of leafy green. Mesclun lettuce might be planted to 4-row beds, while head lettuce might be planted to 2 rows. Some experimentation will be required to see what works best for you.

Scallion/Bunching Onion

Another potentially important high-value crop for SPIN farmers are scallions and bunching onion. Onion sets can be planted throughout the season to produce a steady weekly supply of scallion and onion bunches. There is often a low supply of scallion at farmer's market during the fall season, so if you schedule in some scallion production for this time, you can do very well.

Scallion and bunching onion achieve high-value status under a number of different price/yield combinations as shown in Table 34. Novice SPIN farmers can target 100 units of scallion/bunching onion per week. Expert SPIN farmers can target 1,000 or more units per week. You should be able to get $1 per bunch for your scallion/bunching onion, or $1.50 per bunch if supply is low or demand is high.

> Onion sets can be planted throughout the season to produce a steady weekly supply of scallion and onion bunches.

Table 34: Yield/Price Combinations for Scallion/Bunching Onion

150 bunches of green onion per bed
   a) 50 cents per bunch = $75.00 per standard bed
   b) 75 cents per bunch = $112.50 per standard bed
   c) $1.00 per bunch = $150.00 per standard bed
   d) $1.25 per bunch = $187.50 per standard bed
   e) $1.50 per bunch = $225.00 per standard bed

200 bunches of green onion per standard bed
   f) 50 cents per bunch = $100.00 per standard bed
   g) 75 cents pr bunch = $150.00 per standard bed
   h) $1.00 per bunch = $200.00 per standard bed
   i) $1.25 per bunch = $250.00 per standard bed
   j) $1.50 per bunch = $300.00 per standard bed

Scallion and onion are best planted by hand using onion sets. The rows can be marked with a wheel hoe. Scallion can be planted using 4-6 rows per 2 foot wide bed and 1/2 inch to 1 inch apart in-row. Onion might be planted with 3 - 4 rows per bed, and in-row spacing of 2 - 4 inches.

Radish

Radish can also be considered a high-value crop because supply is often low and that allows you to raise the price. Typically, radish bunches sell better than topped radish. French Breakfast radishes are always winners, as well as the red varieties. Depending on locale, radish can be planted throughout the season to produce a steady weekly supply. Radish can be planted in 4 - 6 row beds, using the Earthway seeder. Seed should be planted around 1/4 inches deep. Table 35 shows the different yield/price combinations for radish.

Table 35: Yield/Price Combinations for Radish

40 bunches per standard bed
    a) 50 cents per bunch = $20.00 per bed
    b) 75 cents per bunch = $30.00 per bed
    c) $1.00 per bunch = $40.00 per bed
    d) $1.25 per bunch = $50.00 per bed
    e) $1.50 per bunch = $60.00 per bed
    f) $2.00 per bunch = $80.00 per bed

50 bunches per standard bed
    g) 50 cents per bunch = $25.00 per bed
    h) 75 cents per bunch = $37.50 per bed
    i) $1.00 per bunch = $50.00 per bed
    j) $1.25 per bunch = $50.00 per bed
    k) $1.50 per bunch = $60.00 per bed
    l) $2.00 per bunch = $80.00 per bed

60 bunches per standard bed
    m) 50 cents per bunch = $30.00 per bed
    n) 75 cents per bunch = $45.00 per bed
    o) $1.00 per bunch = $60.00 per bed
    p) $1.25 per bunch = $75.00 per bed
    q) $1.50 per bunch = $90.00 per bed
    r) $2.00 per bunch = $120.00 per bed

Novice SPIN farmers can target 50 bunches of radish per week. Expert SPIN farmers can target 100 to 500 bunches per week. You should be able to get $1 to $2 per bunch of radish, depending on marketing conditions. Keep in mind that radish is a very quick-growing crop and is usually ready to harvest in less than 30 days. This compensates for it technically not becoming a high value crop as calculated by the yield/price formula.

Carrots

Carrots are another important crop for SPIN farmers. They should be put into production as early in the season as possible. There should also be many subsequent staggered plantings of carrots, which can be done on a relay basis. Carrot bunches can be sold for the first several weeks, followed by bagged carrots. Customers tend to prefer carrot bunches for the first several weeks once carrots are in season, but then would rather buy topped and bagged carrots a little later in the season. If you can be one of the first at market with carrot bunches, then you can do

Customers tend to prefer carrot bunches for the first several weeks once carrots are in season, but then would rather buy topped and bagged carrots a little later in the season.

very well. You might sell up to 500 bunches on a single marketing day.

Carrots can be planted with the Earthway seeder about 1/4 inch deep. You can go over each furrow twice with the seeder, to get in a higher density planting for mini carrots. Early bunching carrots can be planted using a single pass on the seeder. Usually 3 rows per bed are planted. Table 36 shows different yield/price combinations for carrot bunches.

Table 36: Yield/Price Combinations for Carrot Bunches

Targeted Yields of one Bunch per Row Foot; 75 Bunches per Bed
- a) 75 cents per bunch = $56.00 per bed
- b) $1.00 per bunch = $75.00 per bed
- c) $1.50 per bunch = $112.00 per bed
- d) $2.00 per bunch = $150.00 per bed
- e) $2.50 per bunch = $187.50 per bed
- f) $3.00 per bunch = $225.00 per bed

Novice SPIN farmers can target 100 bunches of carrots per week. Expert SPIN farmers, can target 500 bunches per week. You should be able get $2 to $3 per bunch for your bunching carrots.

Mid-sized or Mini Carrots

Higher pricing can be charged for mid-sized or mini carrots. The key to premium pricing is to offer a very well washed product that is bagged, and which looks very clean and appealing when sold at market. Unlike conventional carrots, price levels for mini carrots remain steady throughout the season. Table 37 shows yield/price combinations for smaller-sized carrots.

Table 37: Yield/Price Combinations for Smaller-Sized Carrots

Targeted Yields of .75 lbs. per Row Foot
- a) $1.00 per lb. = $ 56.25
- b) $2.00 per lb. = $112.50
- c) $3.00 per lb. = $168.75
- d) $4.00 per lb. = $225.00
- e) $5.00 per lb. = $281.25

Targeted Yields of 1 lb. per Row Foot
- f) $1.00 per lb. = $ 75.00
- g) $2.00 per lb. = $150.00
- h) $3.00 per lb. = $225.00
- i) $4.00 per lb. = $300.00
- j) $5.00 per lb. = $375.00

Novice SPIN farmers can target 100 one pound bags of mini carrots per week. Expert SPIN farmers can target 300 one pound bags per week. The price range for bagged mini carrots is $2 to $3, and the price for bagged mini carrots remains steady throughout the season.

Potatoes

Potatoes are another highly marketable and popular crop, but are considered a low-value one. If your land base is limited, potatoes should not play a large part in your growing plan. But if your land base is in the 1/2 acre to 1 acre range of production, potatoes can be a fairly important item for you. Early new potatoes sell at high initial prices, and if you harvest early potatoes soon enough in the season you may be able to schedule in another crop, thus making potatoes a possible relay crop. Exotic varieties, such as fingerling and purple fleshed varieties, also sell very well.

SPIN uses the Early-Exotic potato strategy. This involves growing an early variety of potato for your area and selling it at a high price, which provides an opportunity to enhance weekly sales in early summer. Once the price of potatoes starts dropping, you can start marketing exotic gourmet varieties, such as fingerling and purples. High prices for these types of potatoes are usually obtainable throughout the remainder of the growing season. Depending on the size of your operation you might have a few thousand square feet of potatoes in production if your farm is in the 1/4 acre range of production, or you might have up to 10,000 square feet in potato production if your farm is an acre in size. Sub-acre plantings of potatoes can be planted by hand, with two people working together. A wheel hoe can be used to mark the rows. Rows should be at least 3 feet apart, to allow for hilling. Potatoes can be hilled by hand, and potato bugs can be picked off by hand also.

Fresh Herbs

Fresh herbs are excellent additions to your product line, especially the more common ones such as basil, cilantro and baby dill. When selling herbs you can sell them at the same price tier as other items on a mix and match basis. Prices for fresh herbs range from $1.50 to $3 per bunch. Fresh herbs can usually be classed as a high-value crop. Novice farmers might sell 50 or so bunches per marketing week, while more experienced growers might sell several hundred bunches.

Dill seed can be planted with the Earthway seeder using the beets/chard seed plate, with four or five rows per 2 foot wide bed. Cilantro can also be planted with the chard plate, while basil can be planted with the lettuce plate. Herb crops are very easy compared to other crops because they are cut with a knife or scissors and then bundled right in the plot. There is no digging involved, and there is usually no need for washing. Several hundred bunches of herbs can be produced in an hour. You should aim to grow as many fresh herbs as the market will support.

> Once the price of potatoes starts dropping, you can start marketing exotic gourmet varieties, such as fingerling and purples.

Green Beans and Peas

These crops tend to be classed as lower-value ones. But because they are so marketable, they can be quite important for SPIN farms in the 1/2 acre to 1 acre range of production. You can usually get better prices for your green beans and peas if you pre-bag and sell them with other mix and match items at a certain price tier. You can sell beans and peas in ½ to 1 pound quantities at $3 per 1/2 pound bag or 2/$5. Depending on the size of your operation you might sell 50 to several hundred units of these items per marketing week. Harvesting green beans/peas takes time, and work rates vary considerably, but the upside is that these items do not have to be washed.

Beans and peas can be planted with the Earthway seeder, with 2 rows per bed. Soaker hoses placed down the center of the bed are used for irrigation.

> You can usually get better prices for your green beans and peas if you pre-bag and sell them with other items at a certain price tier.

Garlic and Shallots

These are two other important crops to have in the SPIN crop repertoire. They are very marketable crops, especially if you sell your produce at a farmer's market in a large city, and you should be able to sell 50 to 100 bags of these items on a weekly basis. Garlic can be planted in the spring or fall, depending on where you live. Once garlic has matured it is harvested and then cured by air drying. It can then be sold by the head or by the bag. Garlic can be planted by hand in beds. A 2 foot wide bed can contain 3 rows of garlic, with the cloves about 4 to 5 inches apart in the row. Smaller cloves can be planted more intensively to be used as green garlic. Green garlic is an increasingly popular item and can be sold for several marketing weeks. This is garlic that is at an early stage of growth and is bunched like scallion. The green stem and bulb portion are usable. Depending on the size of the farm, SPIN farmers can plant 100-200 pounds of garlic, which can be planted over the course of a few days.

Shallots are another item that is typically in short supply at farmer's markets, but is frequently in high demand. If you can source out a seed supply of shallots, you should plant 100 to 200 pounds in 2-3 row beds with in-row spacing of 8 -12 inches. Once the tops dry back the shallots are taken out of the ground and allowed to air dry for several weeks. They are sold in 1/2 pound mesh bags for $3 per bag.

Cucumbers and Tomatoes

Another crop the SPIN farmer should consider growing is pickling/salad cucumbers. Pickling cucumbers can also be used for salad purposes, and are usually solid sellers at local farmers markets. You should plant a few thousand square feet of cucumbers if you have a larger-sized sub-acre farm. Smaller farms should grow 500 square feet of cucumbers. Trellising can be used to grow cucumbers, and soaker hoses are used for irrigation. Depending on where you grow you might be able to produce cucumbers over 10 marketing weeks. They can be sold in 1/2 pound bags for $3 per bag, and consumers like buying small quantities of this item. Cucumbers can be planted in hills or rows. Plenty of space needs to be left between rows, as the plants will spread out.

Tomatoes can also be grown by SPIN farmers, especially those who live in areas that have long growing seasons. Like cucumbers, they can be produced over 10 or more marketing weeks. Small baskets of tomatoes can be sold for $2 to $3 per basket. Sub-acre farmers also do well with heirloom varieties because they are not available elsewhere, and have a very appreciative following.

The above crops are those that have a place in all SPIN farm growing plans because they provide a solid base of revenue for farmers in most locations. However, there are many more crops and varieties that can be included in your crop repertoire once you get more growing experience and learn what your local market demands. In Guide # 6 you'll learn how to gain control over all the day-to-day farming tasks – fertilizing, prepping plots, planting, watering, managing insects, weeding, harvesting and prepping produce. The SPIN approach to organizing a farm's work flow has saved many a farming career, and it will make you, too, the master of your farming fate.

What Does Wally Grow?

Here is a list of Wally's cash crops. He owes much of his success as a SPIN farmer to them. He's also noted crops he's looking forward to trying. SPIN farmers are always planning ahead!

Spring Crop Repertoire:

Green garlic
Baby red onion bunches
Rhubarb
Salad mix which includes garden grown pea greens, sunflower greens, lettuces, and a variety of garden grown micro greens.
Scallion
Spinach

Looking forward to trying:

Bordeaux spinach: red stemmed
Wally offers most of the spring items during the summer, except spinach, which does not make its reappearance at market until the fall.

Summer/Fall Crop Repertoire:

Beans: green, yellow, broad and fresh shelling varieties
Beets: red, golden and chioggia
Carrots: rainbow carrots (red, purple, white)
Cucumbers
Fresh herbs: basil, cilantro and baby dill
Garlic
Onions (from Dutch onion sets)
Cipollini onions (from seed)
Potatoes: all red, all blue and fingerling
Pumpkins: heirloom varieties
Shallots (from seed)
Tomatoes: heirloom varieties
Winter squash

Looking forward to trying:

Chicory
Eggplant
Charentais melons
Rapini

Winter Crop Repertoire:

Storage crops:

Beets
Carrots: orange and rainbow
Garlic
Onions
Potatoes
Shallots

Wally notes that all of these crops should be highly marketable in most areas. Over time, SPIN farmers develop and streamline their own crop repertoires to suit their own growing and marketing conditions, and that is part of the fun of growing. He urges every SPIN farmer to try their own s-mall p-lot in-troductions, by experimenting with new crops every year. At market, his hands down winners have been rainbow carrots and garden grown pea greens. His biggest flop at market has been Asian greens.

The next logical question is where does Wally buy his seeds? His favorite sources, as well as dozens more hard-to-find and specialty seed companies that come recommended by other SPIN farmers can be found at the SPIN-Farming website - www.spinfarming.com, base camp for SPIN farmers everywhere.

67

SPIN Franchise ready Farming

Think in terms of doing a variety of tasks each day and spreading your harvesting out over an entire week.

SPIN-Farming® Basics

Guide 6: Work Flow Practices

Typical farm tasks…Fertilizing…Prepping plots…Planting…
Watering…Managing insects…Weeding…Harvesting…
Prepping produce…Putting it all together

GUIDE # 6: SPIN-FARMING WORK FLOW PRACTICES

The first 5 Guides introduced the basic concepts of SPIN-Farming. In this Guide, we will outline in more detail how you actually put SPIN into practice.

Typical Farm Tasks

There are a variety of tasks that need to be done on any farm, and unlike conventional farms that employ large work crews, SPIN farmers have to do most, if not all, of the work themselves. It is therefore crucial that you create a regimented and balanced work schedule so that you can manage all of the tasks without becoming overly stressed. The SPIN Five Day Work Week shows you how. Table 38 lists the typical farming tasks.

Table 38: Typical SPIN Farm Tasks
Fertilizing
Prepping plots
Planting
Watering
Managing insects
Weeding
Harvesting
Prepping produce

Once production gets in full swing, the most consuming tasks become harvesting and prepping for market. Produce is usually harvested during the cooler parts of the day, such as in the morning and evening. Weeding and watering tasks can occur during the afternoon, when it usually becomes too warm to harvest and prep many crops.

As has been covered previously, the high-road harvesting technique, which is based on investing in a walk-in cooler, gives you control over the timing of your harvesting tasks. Other important labor-saving tools already mentioned are a rototiller and a garden seeder, which is used to prep and plant beds, and an efficient irrigation system. Weeding is done using hand tools. Most farming tasks must be done on an ongoing basis throughout the growing season, and the following will explain each task in detail and outline the Five Day Work Week.

Fertilizing

SPIN-Farming uses organic-based fertilizers to maintain soil fertility. Sub-acre farms can use inputs that are not practical for large-scale production. For example, fertilizing with composted manure is expensive and impractical on large farms, but it is very feasible for SPIN farms. There are many sources of local materials that can be used as organic fertilizers including bone and blood meal, coffee grounds, composted leaves and grass clippings, fish fertilizer, food industry wastes, oilseed residue such as canola and soybean meal, sea weed based products, wood ash and a variety of other organic compounds. The aim is to use whatever is in abundance locally. If a certain material or fertilizer component is not available locally, then it will certainly be necessary to buy that item, but since the quantities required by sub-acre farms are small, the cost is modest.

If a SPIN farm includes multiple residential locations, composting should occur at each site. The owner of the land is encouraged to set up a composting box, and then the SPIN farmer relies on it for fertilizer purposes. Land owners can recycle grass clippings, leaves, and kitchen wastes, and turn them into valuable inputs for the farm. If practiced extensively in an urban area, SPIN-Farming can contribute significantly to closing the loop on urban-generated organic waste.

SPIN farms can be fertilized in a number of different ways. The entire planting area can be fertilized and then rototilled, or areas can be done on a bed-by-bed basis. In the first instance you might have a plot located in an urban residential backyard. If you plan on exclusively growing potatoes on this plot, you would apply a fertilizer mix of bone and blood meal, composted manure and wood ash. Then you would rototill the area to work in the fertilizer, and plant your crop. This is called area fertilizing, and it is used for a wide range of crops such as beans, garlic, onions, potatoes and shallots.

In other cases, you may decide to fertilize on a per-bed basis. For instance, you might have a few standard size beds that you plan on planting to spinach. Since spinach is a heavy feeder which takes lots of nutrients from the soil, you should apply a little extra nitrogen fertilizer by applying a coffee can of a 50/50 mix of blood meal and coffee grounds to the bed. Once the spinach is harvested, you might relay these two beds to intensively planted green onion, from sets. In this case you simply reapply your fertilizer to the beds after the spinach has been harvested and cleaned up, rototill and then plant the onion sets. Relay cropping often relies on per-bed fertilizing, so you should have plenty of organic materials ready to use throughout the season in order to keep your production consistent.

The SPIN approach to fertilizing relies on common sense and timely additions of inputs. There is no need to spend large amounts of money on organic fertilizer, since you should be relying as much as possible on local organic material, and you should compost as much as you can onsite to limit the amount of off-farm inputs.

> If practiced extensively in an urban area, SPIN-Farming can contribute significantly to closing the loop on urban-generated organic waste.

Prepping Plots

As mentioned above, there are two ways to prep plots in SPIN-Farming. You can prep the entire planting area at one time, or you can prep individual beds. To prep the entire planting area, you simply apply the appropriate inputs and then rototill the area. A rear tine rototiller in the 5 HP to 10 HP range will make quick work of prepping most sub-acre planting areas. You usually set the rototiller tines as deep as they will go, and this will be your planting depth, which might be around 8 inches. Usually you can work a sandy soil deeper than a heavy soil. Also, depending on the soil type, you may have to make more passes with the rototiller to get the appropriate depth. Clay soils usually require more passes than sandy soils.

Bed areas are contained in the intensive relay area and the bi-relay area. In the intensive relay area, the beds will consist of standard size beds, which are beds that measure around 2 feet wide and 25 feet long. It is important to note that beds are "around" 2 feet wide. If you have a 5HP rototiller, your tiller width might be a little narrower than 2 feet. Another type of rototiller might be a little wider than 2 feet. The aim is to have the bed fit the width of your rototiller to make for easy handling. Bed width is also kept to around 2 feet so that the bed can easily be straddled during planting, weeding, and harvesting.

To prep beds, rototill the entire area fairly shallow, around a couple of inches deep. Then use an Earthway wheel hoe and mark a 25 foot long line. This line should be straight. You can 'eyeball' the line using points on a fence. Once you have this line, you place one tire of your rototiller on this line and follow it until you have rototilled a bed 25 feet long. Once you have this first straight initial bed, you then use a wheel hoe and mark off another line 6 to 12 inches from this bed. Once you have this straight line you use your rototiller and make another straight bed. You do this until you have made the required number of beds. Then you can make another pass over each bed with the rototiller to get a little more depth. The bed will now be ready for planting. Eventually you will find that you will not even need to mark off a bed with a wheel hoe, because you will have become adept at making straight beds using your intuition.

You must avoid the home garden practice of relying on strings to mark off straight lines. This technique is cumbersome and takes too much time, especially if you have thousands of square feet to prep and plant. Wheel hoes and line-of-sight reckoning are much quicker. Prepping plots should be done with the idea of reducing as much labor and time as possible.

Planting

A SPIN watering system consists of rubber garden hoses and inexpensive hardware.

Planting, too, must be done as quickly as possible. This is especially relevant if much of your farm is in relay production during the growing season, since most beds are harvested and replanted on an ongoing basis. You can't afford to spend too much time replanting beds, and, as pointed out earlier, the rototiller is an invaluable tool in bed preparation.

A wheeled garden seeder, such as the Earthway garden seeder, is another important tool that greatly reduces the amount of planting time. A standard size bed can be replanted using the seeder in just a matter of minutes.

On some occasions, you will still have to use hand labor when planting crops, such as when planting onion sets or setting out transplants, if you decide to use them in your operation. When planting sets or transplants, you mark off rows with a wheel hoe, and then plant by straddling and moving down the bed. The important point to know now is that planting must be done quickly, and on a timely basis in conjunction with other farm tasks.

Watering

Watering is another farm task that must be done on an ongoing basis throughout the growing season. If you do not have an appropriately designed watering system you will spend too much time with this task. A SPIN watering system consists of rubber garden hoses and inexpensive hardware. Some parts of your farm will have to be watered on a single-set basis. This simply means that you put a watering system in place, and it stays in place during the course of the growing season. When watering many types of crops, you don't want to be dragging garden hoses and repositioning them because it takes too much time and effort. Ideally, the aim is to just turn on the faucet to water your single crop and bi-relay areas. Strip sprinkler attachments and soaker hoses can be bought at local hardware store in 25-and 50-foot lengths. Once you lay them out, your irrigation system is set for the entire growing season.

The watering system for the intensive relay area is designed differently, allowing for easy access to several garden hoses throughout the area. This type of area has many different crops in different stages of growth and maturity so watering such an area in its entirety all at one time is usually not desirable. For instance, within a series of beds you may have just harvested and replanted a few beds. You may therefore just want to quickly soak down these beds for germination purposes, but you may not need to water adjacent beds. So in this case you will hand water using a garden hose and wand attachment. An intensive relay area will also rely on overhead watering with sprinklers, whenever possible.

Soaker hoses are not used in an intensive relay area because too much time would be spent moving the hoses around every time a replanting occurred.

A SPIN watering system must be flexible enough in its design to allow watering with sprinklers and soaker hoses, as well as hoses and wand attachments. When watering plots on a multi-site farm, you also have to be flexible in your approach. If you have to water entire planting areas using a garden hose and wand attachment, you can first go to the plot which has sprinkler irrigation and turn that on so that it is watering while you go to the plot that needs hand watering. This might take you a half hour. Once you are done with the hand watering, you can return to the initial plot and shut off the sprinkler. Multi-site farming requires a bit more creativity and flexibility in watering, but the overall aim is the same: to do it as quickly and efficiently as possible.

Within the framework of the Five Day Work Week, watering is done in conjunction with your harvesting activities. Again, utilizing the high-road harvesting approach with a walk-in cooler will allow you to harvest produce during the week at the most advantageous times, so that watering can then be scheduled on a timely and systemic basis within this context.

It should be said that you may not plan on watering some parts of your farm at all. You might get sufficient rainfall in your locale to effectively grow a wide range of crops without irrigation, so this should be considered when planning your watering system. Not having to water some of your crops, especially when you are growing on a multi-site basis, is very advantageous as it will save you a great deal of time and effort.

> As we have seen with fertilizing, the limited size of sub-acre farms makes an organic approach to insect control feasible…

Managing Insects

As we have seen with fertilizing, the limited size of sub-acre farms makes an organic approach to insect control feasible, and techniques can be applied that would not be possible on large-scale farms. One of the most used SPIN techniques for insect control is hand picking, which is obviously the most environmentally friendly, since it eliminates the use of pesticides. For instance, managing potato bug populations by hand results in two advantages: you save on the cost of an organic pesticide such as rotenone, and beneficial insects are not adversely affected.

Other problem insects, such as leaf miners, can also be controlled by hand picking infested leaves. Hand picking bugs and infected leaves can be done in conjunction with other farming tasks based on the Five Day Work Week, with insect control scheduled during the mid-afternoon when it is too hot to harvest.

Weeding

When it comes to weed control, here, too, sub-acre farmers have an advantage over those with large-scale operations. Weeds are much easier to manage on sub-acre farms and can be done so with hand hoeing equipment and a rototiller when the situation demands it. SPIN-Farming's two important weed control practices are relay cropping and the Four Weeding Strategies. As you have already seen, SPIN utilizes intensive relay cropping, which is based on the planting of quick-growing crops, and then replanting after each harvest. With relay cropping it is frequently not necessary to weed, and when you do need to weed, usually one weeding will be enough. Once a quick-growing crop has been harvested, whatever weeds are remaining will usually not have gone to seed. These weed seedlings can be rototilled in when prepping a bed for the next crop. Over time a relay area will become quite clean of weeds because of this frequent tilling of the soil.

> …2 or 3 hours each week, even for acre-sized farms, should keep walkway areas clear of weeds.

When actual weeding needs to done, the Four Weeding Strategies identify the four distinct parts of the farm that are involved - walkways, between-row areas, in-row, and perimeter areas - and the most effective weed control tools for each.

Table 39 outlines the different weeding strategies for each area of a SPIN farm. A walkway, which is the narrow strip of land, around 6 to 12 inches in width between each bed, can be hoed by hand with a regular garden hoe or a wheel hoe. If many walkway areas need to be weeded out, a small narrow rototiller will do the job. Weeds can also be kept at bay in this area by applying a mulch such as grass clippings. Walkway weeding is easily accomplished, and a certain amount of time is allotted within the Five Day Work Week towards walkway weeding. The amount of time needed, of course, depends on the size of the farm, but 2 or 3 hours each week, even for acre-sized farms, should keep walkway areas clear of weeds.

Table 39: SPIN's Four Weeding Strategies

Walkways:
    Broad hoe, wheel hoe, narrow rototiller, mulching

Between-row areas:
    Bed areas - Collinear and stirrup hoes, narrow specialty cultivators
    Row/walkway areas - Broad hoe, collinear hoe, small rototiller

In-row:
    Handwork

Perimeter:
    Rototiller, broad hoe

After an irrigation or a rainfall, weed seedlings will usually emerge throughout the farm. The first area you should weed is the walkways. Next, you should quickly do a rototilling of your perimeter area. Perimeter areas should take less than 1/2 hour per week, even for acre-sized farms. Once you have your walkways and your perimeter weeded, then you can start weeding out your beds. Beds usually have 2 - 6 rows of crop, depending on what is being grown. The between-row areas are weeded out with a collinear or narrow stirrup hoe.

These hoes draw easily through the soil, as you move down along the bed by working from the walkway. You might go down one side of the bed with your hoe, and then come along the other side of the bed. You should never step in a bed while weeding. All parts of the bed should be within easy and effective reach of your hoe, and indeed this is one of the reasons SPIN-Farming beds are around 2 feet wide. All parts of the bed are easily accessible with a hoe from the walkways that surround a bed.

The amount of time spent doing the between-row weeding in a bed 2 feet wide and 25 feet long should only be a few minutes. If it takes much longer, you are using the wrong tool. Once you do the between-row weeding in a given series of beds, you can then do the in-row weeding. This you do while straddling a bed with your legs. You should be moving at a slow but steady pace down the bed. You don't necessarily have to remove every weed on your initial in-row pass down a bed. You just want to accomplish an initial control. Also, you don't want to spend too much time on any particular bed because you will get behind in weeding the rest of the farm. The main thing is to get in an initial control, and then schedule in subsequent in-row hand weedings, according to your Five Day Work Week schedule. As a rule of thumb, a 1,000 square feet of growing area can be weeded, including the walkways, between-row areas, and the in-row areas, in about 1 hour. This means a 1/4 acre intensive relay area can be effectively weeded in about 10 hours. You don't, of course, do all of this work in one day, but rather you schedule it over the course of the week.

Other areas of the farm can be weeded more quickly. If your farm has a potato area, you can till the between-row areas with your rototiller. Hilling also acts as a weed deterrent.

Other crops in your single crop areas, such as tomatoes and cucumbers, can be quickly weeded because of the wide spacing between the row. Crops in the bi-relay area can also be weeded quickly. Two row beds of peas and beans can be weeded quickly with a collinear hoe. Carrot and onion beds usually require more intensive weeding efforts.

Most farmers lose control of weeds because they don't approach this task with a well-thought out plan. SPIN farmers can guarantee their success at this task by using the Four Weeding Strategies and schedule them within the Five Day Work Week. Steady consistent effort is key.

> Most harvesting tasks can be accomplished with the simplest of tools.

Harvesting

During the growing season, harvesting is one of the most demanding and stressful of all the farming tasks. As has been explained previously, SPIN-Farming distinguishes between two very different approaches to harvesting. One is the high-road, and one is the low-road. The high-road utilizes a walk-in cooler, and the low-road approach does not. SPIN urges you to take the high-road since this gives you control over your harvesting schedule and makes it easier to practice the Five Day Work Week. Harvested produce is stored in the cooler and then can be prepped and bagged at the most opportune time.

Most harvesting tasks can be accomplished with the simplest of tools. A garden fork will do for harvesting potatoes and carrots. A simple kitchen knife is good for harvesting leafy greens. Cheap vinyl or plastic tubs and bins are used for collecting and washing produce. When harvesting, it is important to keep track of your work rate. You should have a stop watch with you at all times during the growing season. This way you can establish your work pace and plan your harvesting activities accordingly. For instance, you may look at ten 50 foot rows of potatoes and think it will take you all day to harvest that area. But if you take a stop watch and time yourself on how long it takes you to harvest a single row, you might discover that it doesn't take you as long as you thought. In this case you might decide to do the work yourself. Or it might take you

Establishing a work pace for each crop that is harvested, and then basing a harvesting schedule on actual work pace is an important component of the Five Day Work Week.

longer than you thought, so you might decide to use your partner to help you harvest this crop. Establishing a work pace for each crop that is harvested, and then basing a harvesting schedule on actual work pace is an important component of the Five Day Work Week.

Prepping Produce

Prepping produce refers to washing and bagging or bunching tasks to get your produce ready for market. The more you clean up and make your produce presentable, the higher the price you can obtain for it. For instance, after harvesting a bed of spinach and placing it in bins, you fill some bins with cool water and wash the spinach. Allow it to drip dry on trays for several minutes, and then take it to the cooler and allow it to dry further. Later on in the day you can bag your spinach. It is best to harvest most leafy greens early in the morning before the heat of the day sets in, while other produce can be harvested during other parts of the day. For instance, beans and potatoes can be harvested in the afternoon. The main aim here is to be able to spread this task out over the course of the week.

Putting It All Together

During the course of a growing season, all farming tasks have to be coordinated so that no one task is too overwhelming, and that all tasks flow smoothly together. Spending too much time on any one part of your operation will mean that another aspect will be neglected. Crops might be lost to weeds, or they might dry up due to lack of watering, or there might not be enough time to harvest them.

So you must create a balance in the overall work flow of your farm. Things tend to get out of balance if you are confined to the low-road approach. If you are overly preoccupied with harvesting your crops during the day or two preceding market then you may be forced to neglect your watering tasks. If you have an inefficient watering system, then you may spend too much time watering and not enough time harvesting and prepping.

Creating the right work flow on your farm is more of an art than a science, but it should again be emphasized that you will have a better chance of creating balance by using the high-road approach, since a walk-in cooler gives you control over when you can harvest your produce. By being able to harvest produce throughout the week, you can avoid concentrating all of your harvesting activities during the day or two preceding market. This eliminates pressure, and balances each day with a variety of tasks. Table 40 gives you an idea of what a work week would look like in mid-summer, when preparing for a Saturday farmers market. The key to SPIN work flow is balance. All tasks have to be accomplished on a weekly and regimented basis.

Table 40: SPIN Work Flow in Mid-Summer Based on High-Road Harvesting

Monday
  6:00 AM to 7:00 AM - Harvest scallions. Place in cooler
  7:00 AM to 7:30 AM - Harvest fresh garlic. Place in cooler
  9:00 AM to Noon - Prep and bunch green onion and garlic. Place in cooler
  1:00 PM to 2:30 PM - Watering
  3:00 PM to 5:00 PM - Weeding
  6:00 PM to 8:00 PM - More weeding

Tuesday
  6:00 AM to 8:00 AM - Harvest carrots
  9:00 AM to Noon - Top carrots
  1:00 PM to 2:30 PM - Wash carrots
  3:00 PM to 4:00 PM - Watering
  4:00 PM to 5:00 PM - Hand pick potato bugs
  6:00 PM to 8:00 PM - Bag carrots
  8:00 PM to 9:00 PM - Weeding

Wednesday
  6:00 AM to 8:00 AM - Harvest and wash radish bunches. Place in cooler
  9:00 AM to Noon - Harvest and wash potatoes
  1:00 PM to 2:30 PM - Replant harvested carrot and radish beds
  3:00 PM to 4:00 PM - Watering
  4:00 PM to 5:00 PM - Weeding
  6:00 PM to 7:00 PM - Bag potatoes
  7:00 PM to 9:00 PM - Harvest green beans. Place in cooler

Thursday
  6:00 AM to 8:00 AM - Harvest lettuce and beets. Place in cooler
  9:00 AM to 10:00 AM - Harvest and wash cucumbers. Place in cooler
  10:00 AM to 11:00 AM - Harvest summer squash. Place in cooler
  11:00 AM to Noon - Harvest beans. Place in cooler
  1:00 PM to 2:30 PM - Watering
  3:00 PM to 4:00 PM - Harvest more beans. Place in cooler
  4:00 PM to 5:00 PM - Replant some harvested beds
  6:00 PM to 7:00 PM - Bag lettuce
  7:00 PM to 7:30 PM - Bag cucumbers
  7:30 PM to 8:00 PM - Bag beans
  8:00 PM to 8:30 PM - Bag summer squash

Table 40: SPIN Work Flow in Mid-Summer Based on High-Road Harvesting

Friday
6:00 AM to 7:30 AM - Harvest, wash, and bag chard. Place in cooler
7:30 AM to 8:30 AM - Harvest fresh herbs. Place in cooler
9:00 AM to Noon - Make flower bouquets. Place in cooler
1:00 PM to 2:30 PM - Watering
2:30 PM to 4:00 PM - Weeding
4:00 PM to 5:00 PM - Load the truck with farm stand gear
Evening - Free time. Get to bed early

Saturday
8:00 AM to 2:00 PM Sell at Market
4:00 PM to 5:00 PM - Watering

Sunday
Weeding and watering tasks. A relaxed day

Table 40 reveals several interesting and telling points. First of all notice that produce was initially harvested on Monday. Most low-road farms don't begin harvesting until Thursday or Friday. Also notice that time is allotted for watering every day of the week, while weeding is done as needed throughout the week. Look at Friday. Doesn't look like an overwhelming day does it? It would be if you took the low-road approach and harvested and prepped produce until midnight. This is where the differences between the high-road and low-road are very apparent. Days prior to market on the high-road are more relaxed. It is just the opposite on the low-road.

In Table 40 the tasks flow in an even manner. Time is also allotted during the week for the replanting of several beds that were harvested. So as you can see, SPIN-Farming relies on a work flow that is not overwhelming and that is easy to accomplish. Notice that you will have to work at least 12 hour days, on most days, except Saturday and Sunday. But keep in mind that eventually you will have an off-season that will give you a chance to take it easy and recoup in preparation for the next farming year.

In Summary

What ties everything together on a SPIN farm is the Five Day Work Week, and the key to creating it is to affect a proper balance among the various farm tasks so that they are all accomplished on a weekly and regimented basis.

In the last guide of this series you'll learn about what for many farmers is an afterthought – marketing. But in the SPIN system, cultivating customers is as important as cultivating crops. In Guide # 7 you will learn all about SPIN's sales and marketing tricks and techniques that will enable you to attract a loyal customer base and generate steady cash flow. You'll see why knowing one's neighbors, building relationships and making community connections are not only a good way to live, but are good for business, too!

SOS: Random Tips from the SPIN Online Support Group

SPIN farmers are known for their resourcefulness and collaborative spirit. Here's just a few of the kinds of tips they regularly share in SPIN's free online email support group.

Raised Beds Without the Lumber

To make raised beds, you can use a walking tractor with an attachment called a Berta Rotary Plow. This can make a raised bed from a grass covered field. This means you could avoid pressure treated wood or worse, railroad ties. No worries about leakage or kids tripping.

Boosting Soil Fertility, Without the Compost (a perennial topic for SPIN farmers)

Compost definitely isn't the only way to prepare your soil for growing vegetables. We knew well in advance that purchasing compost wasn't going to be an economical or convenient option for us, so we relied instead on soil amendments from the local farmer supply store. We used greensand for potassium, rock phosphate for phosphorus, and alfalfa meal for nitrogen. Alfalfa is key - we spread some over the beds before every new relay planting. We are also using green manures - cover crops like clover and rye that add nitrogen to the soil and improve soil structure. The clover will obviate the need for alfalfa meal in the first planting.

For a 1,000 sq. ft. plot, using these methods we might spend about $100 to fertilize it in the first year, and only $20/year after that (since greensand and rock phosphate are effective for a few years).

Surviving a Cold Snap

I just loaned my standard Christmas lights (read "not LED, so warmer") to my neighbor who is concerned about her citrus. She's borrowed my quilt batting and has strung the lights inside the tree wrapped with the batting. Sure beats burning tires.

Flower Power

We're doubling some of our vegetable sales with flower bunches when available. Sunchokes produce a wonderful long-lasting cut daisy, so the plant produces two sources of revenue. The flowers and the roots. Chives and leeks are similar. People love to use the giant green star stems in contemporary arrangements. Unless you're collecting seed, it's a nice way to expand the use of each plant.

Want to join the free SPIN farmers online support group? Email us details about how you are applying SPIN, and we'll sign you up. Our current email addresses are under the Contact us button at www.spinfarming.com.

79

Think in terms of pre-bagged unitized portions that are packaged and priced for convenience.

SPIN-Farming® Basics

Guide 7: Marketing

Creating a farm identity…A few words about organic…
Marketing options…Community supported agriculture
program (CSA)…Restaurant sales…Contract growing…Home
deliveries…Buying clubs…Farm stands…Farmer's markets…
Stand display…Selling your produce…Professional marketing
practices…Mix and match multiple unit pricing

Afterwords

Guide # 7: SPIN-FARMING Marketing

This guide will discuss the major marketing options used by SPIN farmers, including pricing strategies. As has been mentioned previously, one of the keys to successful SPIN-Farming is direct marketing, which means selling directly to the customer or end user, such as a restaurant or caterer. By selling direct, SPIN farmers keep more of their revenue. Direct marketing channels include farmers markets, with a special emphasis on local neighborhood-based ones; community supported agriculture (CSA) programs; small case lot sales to restaurants, caterers, and specialty food shops; home delivery programs; buying clubs; and on site farm stands.

To successfully capitalize on local marketing opportunities, a sub-acre farmer has to adhere to professional marketing practices because they will support getting top dollar for your crops. Price is even more important for a SPIN farm than for larger operations which deal in high volumes. Getting premium prices is not a difficult thing to do as long as you have an understanding of how to position and promote not only your produce, but also yourself and your farm.

Creating a Farm Identity

> To successfully capitalize on local marketing opportunities, a sub-acre farmer has to adhere to professional marketing practices…

Regardless of which sales channels you decide to use, you will first need to develop a farm identity. A farm identity has different components, all of which serve to give customers something unique to remember you by. A graphic presentation of your farm's name provides a logo, and this should appear in all sales literature that you use, both in print or online. Your logo can be creative or straightforward, but you need to decide on one approach and use it consistently. Business cards are a must, and usually form your initial link with a potential customer. Along with your phone number and email, your business card should have your farm logo and your web site address.

A farm name is very important, and it should be one that is simple so that it is easy to remember. Including your first name in it is often a good idea, such as "Susan's Market Garden." People are intrigued with meeting and knowing the producer, and having your first name in your farm name gives the customer something concrete to latch on to. Another option is to base your farm name on something descriptive about the farm's location, like "Forgotten Bottom Farm."

You should also have a web site, and they are getting more and more affordable to set up and operate. The site can be simple or sophisticated, but it should always communicate basic facts about your farm. Farm photos should show your customers what your operation looks like, and they are an important way for customers to identify with what you are doing. They are also important props to have at your farmers market stand, as well as on recipe cards. These all help to create an image of you in the minds of your customers.

If you have a CSA program as part of your operation, you must create a brochure describing how it works, the produce you will be offering, and an easy-to-understand order form. Price lists for restaurants are needed if you are dealing with that market. Having a farm open house is a powerful way of connecting people with your operation, as they get to see local food production up close and personal. Farm visits also offer "proof of concept" regarding the environmental and health benefits of locally grown food. Table 41 outlines all the elements needed to create a farm identity.

Table 41: Elements of Farm Identity

Business cards
CSA brochure
Farmers market signage
Farm name
Farm open houses
Farm photos
Price lists
Recipe cards
Web site

A Few Words About Organic

Many words have been written about the rapid growth and commercialization of the organic movement. Some feel that the term "organic" no longer serves its original purpose, which was to attest to how the produce was grown. The war of words is still raging, but SPIN circumvents the debate entirely with the position that "seeing is believing." That is why a direct connection to the farm and farmer is so important in SPIN marketing. You can explain your vision of farming, and actually show what your techniques are. The more a customer understands and sees, the more loyal, appreciative and trusting they become. And this trustworthiness carries a dollar value for the SPIN farmer because it supports premium prices.

When you sell produce in a local context, people are usually content to hear, and see, that the produce has been grown using recognized organic farming techniques. You can even mention that many of your techniques actually provide environmental benefits above and beyond the requirements of the USDA organic standards. This is especially the case regarding pest management. Because SPIN primarily relies on hand picking to control pests, you can point out that no pesticides are used, not even ones such as rotenone, which is allowable under the USDA standard. Many of your customers will appreciate this, once you bring it to their attention.

Certified organic status makes more sense for large-scale production and distribution, where producers might be located thousands of miles from consumers. But with sub-acre, localized growing and selling it is not necessary or desirable because it creates added expense and hassle. With SPIN-Farming, the most important labels are "home-grown", "locally grown" and "grown naturally without chemicals." Customers are usually willing to pay a premium for locally grown produce that is organically grown, even though it may not be certified organic.

> …this trustworthiness carries a dollar value for the SPIN farmer because it supports premium prices.

Marketing Options

Some farmers use only one sales channel, such as a CSA program, while others have a diversified sales base.

When it comes to selling your produce locally there are several direct marketing options to choose from. Some farmers use only one sales channel, such as a CSA program, while others have a diversified sales base. Each farmer has to determine which sales channels make sense for them. Perhaps the best option for the novice is the local farmers market. If you don't have a farmers market within a reasonable distance, you can consider other options. Many restaurants are interested in purchasing high-quality locally grown produce, and you might find several that would commit to buying produce from you. A CSA program is another option. Buying clubs are similar to CSA sales. Home deliveries based on web or phone ordering systems are another option. Having an on site farm stand is also a good option, especially if you are a rural farmer. Table 42 shows SPIN's major marketing options.

Table 42: SPIN Direct Marketing Options
Farmers market-Good for novices
Farm stand-Good for novices
Home deliveries-Good for novices
Buying clubs-For experienced growers
CSA program-For more experienced growers
Restaurant sales-For more experienced growers

If you are farming close to or in an urban environment you can tap into all of the options listed in Table 42. As has been pointed out previously, urban farmers located right in the midst of many potential buyers of produce have a marketing advantage over their rural counterparts.

Community Supported Agriculture Program (CSA)

CSA sales can be an important part of many SPIN farms. The CSA concept offers a loose framework, and each farm can structure it differently to satisfy both the needs of the farmer and the members. Typically a farm offers weekly food boxes or "shares." Members sign up typically before the season begins in January through March, and pay at least part of the farm's start-up costs each year. Subscriptions usually start in the $500 range, so even a small list of subscribers can generate a substantial amount of income for your farm.

Food is harvested each week through the growing season, typically May through October, and the farm staff and volunteer members divide the food into boxes. Members then either pick up their box at the farm or from some convenient drop-off point. Some CSA programs allow members to come on the farm each week to harvest their own produce.

CSA's were initially conceived as an alternative to the increasing globalization and mechanization of foods systems which work against independent farmers, puts great strain on the environment and wastes immense quantities of food. Because the mass production-based food system is so impersonal and complicated, it causes many consumers to be suspicious about their produce and uncomfortable with the consequences of growing it. The "sharing of the risk" in the partnership between the consumer and farmer mitigates most of the headaches of modern farming: the need to scrape up capital, fear for an income and the threat of bankruptcy. Rather than scrambling for market share to stay in business, the farmer enjoys the stability that comes from satisfying customers directly.

Like all great ideas, CSA's seem to have caught on in several places throughout the world at once. There are accounts of community farm initiatives in Japan and Chile in the early 1970's. The ideas that inspired the first two American CSA's came from farms in Switzerland and Germany. Indian Line Farm in Massachusetts and Temple-Wilton Community Farm in New Hampshire, both launched in 1986, and are still in operation. So CSA has over a 20 year history in America, and it is particularly compelling now, with vast amounts of farmland being lost and food safety and security becoming more pressing concerns.

It should be noted that a CSA program is based on producing a steady supply of produce for your subscribers on a weekly basis throughout the growing season. To be able to do this you need to be a fairly accomplished grower. If you feel confident you can manage consistent production, then you should by all means consider implementing a CSA program.

Restaurant Sales

Many SPIN farms tap into the sizeable restaurant market. It should be mentioned from the outset that, like CSA sales, restaurant sales should only be considered by experienced farmers. Restaurants expect quality and continuity of production. For instance, you might be able to get a local restaurant interested in buying your salad mix, but you need to have the growing skills that will allow you to deliver salad mix on a week after week basis during the growing season. Restaurants will have some tolerance for production gaps, but the more consistent you can be in your production the better will be your relationship with the restaurant. That being said, there are significant opportunities available for sub-acre farmers in terms of restaurant sales.

Upscale restaurants are often interested in salad greens, and you should be able to make significant weekly sales for many marketing weeks. Restaurants are also interested in baby carrots, exotic vegetables such as chioggia and golden beets and fingerling potatoes. Restaurants are used to buying their produce in case lot quantities, so SPIN farmers need to be prepared to sell to them on that basis. For instance, you can sell salad mixes in case lot quantities of nine1/2 pound bags at a cost of $20 per case. Other produce items can be sold on a case lot basis also. Buying and selling in case lots makes it easier for the chef to order, and for you to organize your harvesting and packing.

If you farm in the city, selling to restaurants can become an important part of your business. Since you live close to many restaurants, often only a few minutes drive, it becomes feasible to make many small deliveries throughout the week. Rush orders can be filled easily. Restaurants like this sort of responsiveness, and they also can purchase any over-production of items that you might have.

Average single orders for a restaurant might be in the hundred dollar range, depending on its size and type. For instance, small restaurants might buy 2 or 3 cases of salad mix. Larger restaurants would order significantly more. If you are having success with restaurant sales you could consider specializing more of your production towards this sales channel. As a SPIN farmer you can easily adjust production to suit the demands of several restaurant clients.

> It should be noted that a CSA program is based on producing a steady supply of produce for your subscribers on a weekly basis throughout the growing season.

Contract Growing

Another option to consider is growing produce on a contractual basis for a restaurant. You could grow specialty items such as chioggia and golden beets, or fingerling potatoes or gourmet baby carrots, and sell them to a contracted restaurant on a weekly basis during the growing season, once those items come on stream. You could also keep them in storage and have them ready for delivery whenever your restaurant calls. Contract growing is a good option for anyone who does not have access to a farmers market, or who is interested in participating in the restaurant industry.

Home Deliveries

Home deliveries require that you have a variety of produce available for sale throughout the growing season.

Another option for SPIN farmers to consider is home deliveries. This simply means you make deliveries of produce to your customers. Standard operating components of this type of sales channel include a business card made up with the name of your operation, your phone number, e-mail address, and web site address. You also need a web site to build up your local profile, inform the public of what your operation is all about and list your product line.

Home deliveries require that you have a variety of produce available for sale throughout the growing season. Once a person expresses interest in your farm, they simply send you an e-mail saying that they would like to receive an e-mail update throughout the growing season regarding what you have for sale. A minimum size of order for a home delivery is set, perhaps at $20.00, or even more, depending on your market.

This sales channel is ideal for urban farmers because they do not need to drive great distances to service their network of customers. Having a few dozen, or more, of these types of deliveries each week can represent a substantial source of revenue, and are perfect if you are a novice grower, uncertain about the timelines of your harvest. When produce is available, you can update your customers by e-mail. Home deliveries can compliment farmers market sales, and both use the mix and match multiple-unit pricing strategy which will be explained later in this guide, and which is a very powerful marketing tool.

Buying Clubs

Yet another option to consider is a buying club, which requires the creation of a web-based ordering system. The concept is similar to a CSA in that customers deposit an upfront fee into an account. Each week a list of items is e-mailed to them, and they place their order off the list. Their account is then debited according to the cost of their weekly order. They then pick up their order from a central drop-off point. When their balance gets below a certain amount, they make another deposit to their account. This is a variation on the CSA, with each order being tailored to each customer's needs.

Farm Stands

SPIN farmers can also set up a farm stand on site, or possibly at a nearby roadside. Whenever you have produce available you can set up your stand and have a sign indicating that you have produce for sale. This is a good option for rural farmers who live close to busy highways, but it can also work for urban farmers.

Farmers Markets

Local farmers markets are among the most lucrative ways to sell produce for both novice and experienced SPIN farmers. Farmers markets also provide an excellent opportunity for novices to get a read on the market. They will see for themselves what sells and what doesn't, or when certain types of produce are in low supply and high demand at market. Novice growers also learn to become consistent growers, as they gear production towards weekly sales.

Many consumers and producers don't have a clear idea of exactly what a farmers market is. Many larger urban centers have a public market such as Granville Island in Vancouver or Reading Terminal Market in Philadelphia, where produce is sold by an assortment of vendors. In these types of markets most of the produce vendors are simply reselling produce that has been purchased from wholesalers or from an actual farm. So the person or operation involved with the selling of the produce is not the farmer who grew it. Usually the sources of this produce are large-scale farming operations that receive subsidies and are located hundreds of miles away from the market. Prices are therefore frequently lower than what is needed to sustain the locally-based sub-acre farmer.

A true farmers market, which most cities and many towns have, is one where the farmer is the seller of the produce. It is these markets that are most appropriate for SPIN farmers because prices at these markets are in line with what a sub-acre farmer needs to support their kind of operation. Novice farmers may at first feel intimidated by other growers who have large, multi-acre farms in the country. Don't be. What you will discover once you start SPIN-Farming is that you can leverage many advantages over larger growers, especially if you are an urban farmer.

Micro climate advantages associated with growing in the city are very real. You should be able to get to market with early spring produce before growers in the country, and you might have a longer frost free fall than growers in the country. In addition, many country growers have problems growing certain types of crops such as lettuce, and you might be able to establish yourself as a significant steady supplier of certain crops that are in frequent short supply at your farmers market. Also, you can top off supplies if you sell out of an item in advance of a market's closing by returning to your farm and harvesting and prepping and returning to market with the sold out item. So you will discover that, although your operation is small, you can establish yourself as an important player at your local farmers market.

> Customers notice when you make the extra effort to keep your produce in good condition.

Stand Display

A market stand need only consist of four or five 2 foot by 4 foot folding tables arranged along the perimeter of your allotted space at your market. Inexpensive tablecloths and woven or plastic baskets are important and inexpensive accessories. Attractive signage can be made with your computer. Produce should be iced during the day to keep its appearance, especially during hot conditions. Many vendors at farmers markets don't use ice, so if you do use ice, you can expect extra sales on this account. Bunches of scallion and radish can be kept cool by placing them on ice packs, and sprinkling them with crushed or cubed ice, which can be made at home, or bought. Customers notice when you make the extra effort to keep your produce in good condition. It is also important to interact with potential customers. It costs you nothing to be pleasant and outgoing. People need to be made aware or your operation, and why you are excited about what you are selling. You'll be surprised at how contagious excitement can be, and an excited customer is a motivated customer.

Selling Your Produce

Many farmers bring a scale to market and sell all, or most, of their produce loose, out of bins, with the customer placing the items in a bag, which is then weighed. There are several things wrong with this approach. First of all, it takes more time to service a customer with this method. Once a customer places a certain quantity of an item in a bag they may ask you to weigh it to see how much it will cost, and then ask to add or take out produce from the bag. This all takes time. If you are having a busy day at market, a line starts forming at your stand, and you might start losing customers as they get frustrated with waiting.

Offering produce in bins, loose, and on a per pound basis, encourages customers to become overly price conscious. If given this option, many customers may choose to only buy small quantities of items, thus limiting the amount of money they spend at your stand. SPIN farmers use professional marketing practices to get their customers to spend as much as possible at their stands.

Consumers are visually oriented when it comes to buying produce…

Professional Marketing Practices

Professional marketing practices all aim to get a customer to spend money freely at your stand, without getting focused on the actual per pound price. They are also a valuable competitive tool since many other farmers disregard them.

Consumers are visually-oriented when it comes to buying produce, so your produce must be very clean when it is sold at your market stand. Setting up and using an effective post-harvesting station at your farm is therefore important to being able to market effectively. The work can be very tedious and labor intensive, such as taking baby carrots through several washes, but it is worth the effort because it will allow you to get high prices for your produce at market. Keep in mind that if you take the high-road harvesting approach by incorporating a walk-in cooler into your operation, you will be bringing to market much higher quality produce than those farmers who do not use one. A walk-in cooler removes the field heat from produce and keeps it in good physical condition until you bring it to market. Also, it keeps produce in better condition longer than if it had not been stored in a cooler.

Clean, high-quality produce is the starting point in SPIN farmers' efforts to get top dollar for their produce. And to get even higher prices, they pre-bag their produce into discrete units. For instance, you might place a 1/2 pound of salad mix into a bag, or 1 pound of green beans, or 2 pounds of potatoes, or 1 pound of baby carrots. The idea is to pre-bag or basket your items, using whatever unit weight you feel is appropriate, and then to sell these items on a mix and match multiple-unit basis.

You may already be familiar with multiple-unit pricing as many large supermarkets use this method. And here is one area where SPIN farmers take a tip from the big guys. The idea is to offer a customer a price break over the single unit price, if they buy multiple quantities. For instance, a single item might be $1.50, but if you buy 3 units you pay only $4.

The idea is to get the customer to buy more by giving them a per unit price break. If you look around at your local farmers market there is a good chance very few, if any, growers use this technique. This goes to show how far farmers have to go in terms of getting better at marketing their produce.

Using multiple-unit pricing for your produce will usually translate into more sales at your stand. Here's how. If you tried selling your mesclun mix for $5 per pound, you might turn off many customers who think they are paying an exorbitant price. But if you put a 1/2 pound of salad mix in a bag, and then sell the bags for $3 per bag, or 2 for $5, consumer resistance to buying your produce is immediately broken down. A consumer does not mind spending $5 if they know exactly what they are getting, and since your salad mix is pre-bagged, they can pick up a bag and see if they are happy with the quantity of produce they are getting. Also, chances are if they like what they see, they will probably go for the multiple-unit quantity, and buy 2/$5. It's just the way the consumer thinks. Also, if all of your produce is sold this way, you will be able to move customers a lot faster. A customer can just grab a couple of bags and throw a five dollar bill your way, and the transaction only takes a few seconds. A quickly-serviced customer is a happy customer, and a good reflection on you.

> Using multiple-unit pricing for your produce will usually translate into more sales…

Mix and Match Multiple-unit Pricing

If you have 10 different produce items for sale and use 10 different multiple-unit pricing combinations, then you are apt to confuse the customer. Instead, you should sell those 10 items at the same price and then offer them for sale on a mix and match multiple-unit basis. This means a customer can choose any mix of items and get the same multiple-unit price break. For instance, Table 43 shows how you might sell the following items at market all at the same price, but with the amount of produce varying, depending on the item.

Table 43: A Mix and Match Multiple-unit Price Offering in Mid-summer
All items $3.00 per bag or any 2/$5.00
1/2 lb. bags of salad mix
1 lb. bags of baby carrots
1 lb. bags of chard
1 lb. bags of green beans
1 lb. bags of peeled onion
2 lb. bags of cucumber
2 lb. bags of potatoes
large red or golden beet bunches

As you can see in Table 43, a wide variety of items in different weights and sizes are all sold at the same price. The customer can choose any two items for $5. Several things happen when you use this price scheme. For one thing, the customer immediately starts thinking about which two items they want to choose. And since they know exactly what they will be getting for $5, they usually have no problem spending $5. And, they will more than likely buy more than $5 worth of produce, and will usually buy some multiple of $5, such as $10, $15, or $20. In other words, they are more likely to spend money more freely at your stand if you use this price scheme, than if you simply offer your produce loose by weight.

…when you use
this price scheme it
helps a great deal
if you engage the
customer.

It should be mentioned that when you use this price scheme it helps a great deal if you engage the customer. By the end of the day at market, your voice should be nearly hoarse from your mentioning to customers that you are offering your produce on a mix and match basis. Tell them they can have any 2 items for $5, over and over. Customers are frequently slow to catch on, especially since mix and match pricing is not customary among other farmers, so you really need to engage them on this point.

You can also sell produce using mix and match multiple-unit pricing by using different price tiers. Some produce items, such as scallions, radish bunches, and fresh herbs are best sold at lower unit prices than items such as salad green and bags of carrots. So you might consider having 2 price tiers for your produce, as illustrated in Table 44.

Table 44: A 2 Price Tier Market

These items are $1.50 per bunch or any 3/$4.00
Arugula bunches
Dill
Green garlic
Parsley bunches
Radish bunch
Scallion
These items are $3.00 per item or any 2/$5.00
1 lb. bags of carrots
Bunches of chard
3 lb. bags of potatoes
Bags of summer squash
Bags of cucumbers

Having 2 price tiers makes it possible to sell most of your produce at one or the other price. It is not recommended to have more than 2 price tiers, as it can get confusing for the customer. Items at different price tiers are put at different locations on your tables at your market stand, with the lesser priced items on one side, and then the higher priced items on the other.

In Summary

This guide has outlined the most important aspect of farming besides being a good grower. You also need to be a good marketer, because there is no sense growing delicious, nutritious food if you can't get anyone to buy it. That's why you should research and plan which direct marketing options you intend to use, and how you are going to price your produce, before you even put a shovel in the ground. Since there is no one single right plan for all farmers, you will have to explore all of your options. A CSA program might be the best choice for one SPIN farmer, while another will have better success selling solely at farmers markets. What all the SPIN marketing options have in common is that they are based on knowing one's neighbors, building relationships and making community connections.

EYE CANDY

"Mixed veggie packs sell very well at market. White, orange and purple cauliflower buds, about 1.25 lb can go for $5/bag. You can also mix broccoli buds and cauliflower, or snap peas with carrots, or cauliflower and carrots. Or try a 'stir-fry' pack – Raab broccoli, green onion, pea shoots, radishes and mustard greens. Leave the top of the bag open with the greens coming out of the top a bit. I have also sold radish flower buds for $2.50 a bundle, called it spicy wild broccoli for stir-frying."
– Jackie Milne, Hay River, Northwest Territories

Here's what SPIN farmers talk about »

SPIN-Farming® Basics

Afterwords

Lexicon
Mindset
Community
Calculator

Lexicon

SPIN-Farming has its own unique techniques and language. To help get your head around how SPIN differs from conventional farming methods, or from home gardening, here's a translation of the important terms you'll hear when you find yourself in a room full of SPIN farmers.

Sub-acre land base — SPIN transfers commercial farming techniques to sub-acre land bases. Farmers do not need to own much, or any land, to start their operations, and they can be single or multi-sited.

Structured work flow practices — SPIN outlines a deliberate and disciplined day-by-day work routine so that the wide variety of farm tasks can be easily managed without any one task becoming overwhelming.

High-road/Low-road — SPIN distinguishes between two different harvesting techniques. High-road utilizes commercial refrigeration equipment. Low-road harvesting does not.

High-value crops — SPIN devotes most of its land base to the production of high-value crops, defined as ones that generate at least $100 per crop/per bed.

Relay cropping — SPIN calls for the sequential growing of crops in a single bed throughout a single season.

Intensive relays — 3 or 4 crops per season are grown.

Bi-relays — 2 crops per bed per season are grown.

Single crops — 1 crop per bed per season is grown.

1-2-3 bed layout — Refers to the 3 different areas of a SPIN farm devoted to the different levels of production intensity.

75/25 land allocation — Dictates how much land is assigned to the different levels of productionon a SPIN farm. The aim is to balance production between high-value and low-value crops to produce a steady revenue stream and to target revenue based on farm size. The smaller the land base the more of it can be devoted to intensive relay production.

Farm layout — SPIN provides guidelines for segmenting a land base into a series of beds, separated by access alleys, which are small 2 feet strips, just wide enough for a rototiller. An acre accommodates approximately 480 standard size beds, including the necessary paths and access alleys. SPIN can also incorporate more traditional approaches to land allocation.

Standard size beds — SPIN utilizes beds measuring 2 feet wide by 25 feet long.

Revenue targeting formula — By growing high-value crops worth $100 per harvest per bed, and by practicing intensive relay cropping which produces at least 3 crops per bed per season, SPIN targets at least $300 in gross sales per bed per season. With approximately 480 beds per acre, the maximum revenue potential is 480 beds x $300 per bed per season = $144,000 gross sales per acre. When farming is approached in terms of beds instead of acres, the result is a very precise idea of how much growing space can be utilized, and how that space can be managed to generate predictable and steady income.

Organic-based — SPIN relies on all-organic farming practices. There are minimal off-farm inputs and very little waste.

Crop Diversity — A SPIN product line contains a very wide diversity of crops, with some SPIN farms producing over 100 different varieties and 50 different types of crops per season. However, SPIN also provides models that specialize in a particular crop.

Season extension is optional — SPIN does not rely on season extension to expand production; however season extension can be utilized to push SPIN yields and income significantly higher.

Direct marketing — SPIN bases crop selection on what local markets want. Being close to markets allows for constant product feedback and ensures a loyal and dependable customer base. Grow what you sell, don't sell what you grow, is the SPIN farmer's mantra.

Mix and match multiple unit pricing — SPIN's marketing approach is to pre-bag produce items and sell them at certain price tiers — for example, $3.00/unit or any 2 for $5.00.

Commercial refrigeration capacity — SPIN calls for taking the "high-road" by utilizing commercial refrigeration capacity because cooling crops immediately after they are harvested retains their quality which supports premium pricing. It also provides control over the harvest schedule and allows for a manageable work flow.

Minimal mechanization and infrastructure — SPIN's most important and costly equipment are a rototiller and a walk-in cooler or upright produce cooler. All other SPIN implements and infrastructure can be sourced at local garden supply or hardware stores.

"Home-based" work crew — Supplemental labor requirements for a SPIN farm are minimal and can be readily obtained within the network of family, friends, or within the local community.

Utilization of existing water sources — SPIN relies on local water service or wells for all of its irrigation needs.

Low capital intensive — Minimal infrastructure and minimal overhead keeps SPIN farm's start-up and operating expenses manageable. The bottom line is little or no debt.

The more you use the lexicon, the clearer these concepts become. Pretty soon, you find yourself thinking like a SPIN farmer >>>

DIY SEED BOXES

"I have always grown my indoor seedlings in wooden boxes lined with 7 sheets of newspaper. We were in need of new boxes so here is how we went about it. We acquired free oak pallets that were not treated with anything. They tend to be a bit splintery so be careful when handling them. Then we took the skill saw and cut 4 lengths @ 22" and 2 lengths @ 8". The reason for cutting the lengths right from the pallet is because if you attempt to break a pallet apart the wood gets damaged so cutting the lengths directly from the pallet is the way to go. Then the assembly is easy....2 long sides and 2 short sides with the remaining 2 long boards for the bottom with a large enough slit in the middle to allow the passage of water. Then you line the box with 7 sheets of newspaper (no color if possible), fill it with soil and away you go."
— Linda Borghi, Abundant Life Farm, Walker Valley, NY

Here's what SPIN farmers think about »

SPIN-Farming® Basics

Afterwords

Lexicon
Mindset
Community
Calculator

Mindset

SPIN-Farming provides a conceptual framework, or mindset, that helps you navigate the world of commercial growing in general, and sub-acre farming specifically. Here are some sub-acre farming advantages to start putting you in the SPIN frame of mind.

Small timely plantings: These result in a more diverse crop repertoire. More diversity translates into a steady cash flow and minimizes the damage from any one crop failure.

Market responsiveness: As your season progresses you can make mid-course adjustments in your crop plan based on customers' feedback on what they'd like more or less of, or what they want but can't find. It is almost like growing on contract, without the contract.

Market proximity: Sub-acre farming can be located closer to markets, reducing transportation time and costs.

Micro climate effects: Smaller plots give you more options on how you site your operation. By siting it an area protected from wind or in an urban setting, the plots warm up sooner and retain heat longer, allowing you to get into production earlier and extending production later into the season.

Lower expenses: Examples of sub-acre farming's lower expenses include: using a personal vehicle as a farm vehicle – a cargo van or mini-truck is adequate in size for sub-acre scale farming; creating an irrigation system from standard grade garden hoses; using minimal mechanization; relying on local sources of supply for fertilizer which eliminates the use of chemicals; using a simple post-harvesting setup. The aim with SPIN-Farming is to keep expenses at 10% to 20% of total sales.

Minimal outside labor: Labor is the single biggest expense in any operation. Sub-acre scale farming minimizes or even eliminates the need for outside labor, and it very much carries on the tradition of using the low-cost/no-cost network of family and friends during peak labor times.

Partnership with Nature: It's much easier to turn Nature into a co-operative business partner at a sub-acre scale by using inexpensive organic-based processes for pests and weed control and fertilizing that would be impractical for larger operations.

Beautification: Being a small operation, it's much easier to produce shock and awe by making your farm visually pleasing. Considering you may have near-by neighbors, aesthetics are important. Perimeter landscaping, well-maintained plots, flowers in production all will create farms that are nothing short of utopian. Your farm's appearance also says something about you. The surest way to impress someone, be it customers or the community, is to create a farming landscape that borders on the sublime. Good-looking farms tend to be good-earning farms, too.

Identity: Perhaps the most important aspect of the SPIN mindset is that it leads to a collective view of the world that in turn fosters a professional identity that independent small scale growers haven't had before. This identity confers purpose, legitimacy and an economic value on what up until now has been dismissed as quaint, backwards or inconsequential.

And that leads to the question: So what are you?
Part of something bigger than you may realize. >>>

EMAIL MARKETING

"For beginners, I would recommend a "reverse CSA" — an email harvest or e-farmers market. I have been doing this successfully for about 2 years now. I send out an email of what I have and the price. The people on the email list choose what they want and send it back to me. I have made it very clear to them that I will NOT always be able to fill their order, although I try to be fair and give everyone something. This is a great learning tool also as you will find out very quickly what people want and the price they are willing to pay. As you see these trends in your list, you can plant accordingly. "
— Theo, Morrison, The Neighborhood Farm, Maui, HI

So is this a movement? »

SPIN-Farming® Basics

Afterwords

Lexicon
Mindset
Community
Calculator

Community

SPIN Farmers Have Been Called Many Things...

Sub-acre farmers...Neo-agrarians...Hobby farmers...Craft farmers...Micro-farmers...Self-made farmers...Citizen-farmers...The farmers next door...Foolish amateurs...Really big gardeners...Food entrepreneurs.

Whatever you call yourself, you are part of an exuberant, expanding people-to-people experiment whose contributors thrill to the notion that they are engaging in something historical and momentous.

Whether they establish their farmsteads in the middle of urban jungles or sprawling suburbia, SPIN farmers are all uniting behind engaged, rather than escapist, agriculture. They are returning to the cities and towns that have segregated food production beyond their borders, and re-introducing the practice of intelligent, dedicated, craft and soil-based farming. They are making food production visible and palatable and galvanizing their neighbors around an activity that delivers both economic and environmental benefits. And they are bringing the well-documented redemptive power of agriculture to their communities in a commercially viable manner.

By re-casting farming as a small business in a city or town, they are defining progress not by "more and bigger" but by "healthy and balanced." They are showing how to make more from less, how to live large, yet be small, and they are leading a farming revival that cuts across geography, generations, incomes and ideologies to provide common ground, quite literally, beneath everyone's feet.

So Is This A Movement?

Join In!

Whatever it is, you can join in at www.spinfarming.com, where SPIN farmers go to stock up on provisions for both the material and contemplative sides of farming, and where you can:

FIND additional guides in the SPIN-Farming learning series for purchase and immediate access online. Case studies of different scales of operation and of farms that specialize in particular crops give you models to follow in starting your own operation.

SHARE in the success stories of fellow SPIN farmers.

VISIT the gallery to see what life is like down on the SPIN farm.

VIEW free pass-alongs that provide snapshots of SPIN gear, techniques, crops and lifestyle.

USE an online directory of suppliers recommended by your fellow SPIN farmers.

JOIN the free SPIN farmers online support group by emailing us a brief description of how you are applying SPIN. We'll be glad to welcome you among some of the brightest new minds in farming who are problem-solving in an environment that offers just the right mix of freedom and rigor, objectivity and passion. It's a collaborative mechanism for both self-improvement and for contributing enhancements to the SPIN system. Our most up-to-date contact information can be found under the "Contact us" button at www.spinfarming.com.

So tell us...what's your vision?

TWO TIERED CSA

I'm a beginning SPIN farmer in St. Louis Missouri, and I have no experience farming or marketing in this or any channel, but this is an idea I've been thinking about. You could do a two tiered CSA. One tier of the CSA (middle class people) could purchase "sponsorship shares," which would then offset the cost of healthy food for the other tier, low-income people in your or their community. Just as an example: Let's say you're selling shares for an average of $500, which would be a $20 box for 25 weeks. You could reduce the price to $12 a box in the economically depressed community, if the other tier is willing to pay $28 a box or a $700 dollar share. One tier could pay upfront and the other tier could pay weekly. I think this type of service is: 1) good for everybody; 2) let's you reach more people closer by and 3) is very marketable to church communities as a very direct way they can help people and the health of their community. You could make some presentations in Churches in your 25,000 person town 40 min. away and see who's interested. Then you would also have very convenient CSA drop-off points. And then you could hook up with a local social service agency and see if they have clients who need this type of help.
— Alicia Michels, St. Louis, MO

See what's possible, do what's practical »

SPIN-Farming® Basics

Afterwords

Lexicon
Mindset
Community
Calculator

Lot size = 20,000 sq.ft. (about a 1/2 acre)

1/2 acre low end value of production: 240 beds × $100 = $24,000 gross

1/2 acre high end value of production: 240 beds × $300 = $72,000 gross

SPIN revenue potential on 1/2 acre is: $24,000 – $72,000 gross

Once you put on **SPIN** glasses, you start seeing dollar signs all over vacant and underutilized patches of land. To project what all that land is worth in sub-acre farming revenue, all you need is the back of an envelope and the computer between your ears! Here is the calculation for figuring out how much that lot up the street, down the corner or around the block is worth in food production, when **SPIN-Farming** takes root there.

Farm Income Calculator

1. Figure out how many square feet the space represents

2. Figure out how many standard size beds, which measure 2 feet wide by 25 feet long, fit into the space, using this guideline: Number of standard size beds per 20,000 sq. ft. (1/2 acre) = 240

3. Figure out the low end revenue potential of the space by multiplying the number of beds by $100, which is the revenue generated by **SPIN-Farming**'s single crop production

4. Figure out the high end revenue potential of the space by multiplying the number of beds by $300, which is the revenue generated by **SPIN-Farming**'s intensive relay crop production

So how much farm income can you get from your lot?

Make It Happen!

My Lot Size:

Number of standard size beds:

Low end production value:

High end production value:

Farm Income Calculator

1. Figure out how many square feet the space represents

2. Figure out how many standard size beds, which measure 2 feet wide by 25 feet long, fit into the space, using this guideline:
   Number of standard size beds per 20,000 sq. ft. (1/2 acre) = 240

3. Figure out the low end revenue potential of the space by multiplying the number of beds by $100, which is the revenue generated by **SPIN-Farming**'s single crop production

4. Figure out the high end revenue potential of the space by multiplying the number of beds by $300, which is the revenue generated by **SPIN-Farming**'s intensive relay crop production

Join In!

Regardless of where your SPIN farm takes root, join us at www.spifnarming.com. It's home base for SPIN farmers everywhere!

See what's possible...

Do what's practical...

About the Authors

Wally Satzewich

Wally Satzewich and Gail Vandersteen operate Wally's Urban Market Garden which is a multi-locational sub-acre urban farm. It was originally dispersed over 25 residential backyard garden plots in Saskatoon, Saskatchewan, that were rented from homeowners. The sites range in size from 500 square feet to 3,000 square feet, and the growing area totals a half-acre. The produce is sold at The Saskatoon Farmers Market and restaurants in the city.

Wally and Gail initially started farming on an acre-size plot outside of Saskatoon 20 years ago. Thinking that expanding acreage was critical to their success, they bought some farmland adjacent to the South Saskatchewan river 40 miles north of Saskatoon where they eventually grew vegetables on about 20 acres of irrigated land. The farmland was considered an idyllic farming site on its riverfront location. However, the crops were perpetually challenged by wind and hail, insect infestation, rodents and deer. Fluctuating water levels inhibited irrigation during dry spells. "We still lived in the city where we had a couple of small plots to grow crops like radishes, green onion and salad mix, which were our most profitable crops. We could grow three crops a year on the same site, pick and process on-site and put the produce into our cooler so it would be fresh for the market," Gail says.

After six years farming their rural site, the couple realized there was more money to be made growing multiple crops intensively in the city, so they sold the farm and became urban growers. Growing vegetable crops in the city was less complicated than mechanized, large-scale farming. They used to have a tractor to hill potatoes and cultivate, but they discovered it's more efficient to do things by hand. Other than a rototiller, all they need is a push-type seeder and a few hand tools.

They have recently expanded their multi-locational vegetable and flower gardens in the hamlet of Pleasantdale,Saskatchewan which will serve as the home base for training programs on sub-acre farming.

"We're trying to open up farming to a lot of different people that might not have seen it as possible for them."

Wally points out that urban growing provides a more controlled environment, with fewer pests, better wind protection and a longer growing season. "We are producing 10-15 different crops and sell thousands of bunches of radishes and green onions and thousands of bags of salad greens and carrots each season. Our volumes are low compared to conventional farming, but we sell high-quality organic products at very high-end prices." The SPIN-Farming method is based on Wally's successful experiment in downsizing and emphasizes minimal mechanization and maximum fiscal discipline and planning.

Brian Halweil, a food issues writer and researcher at the Washington-DC-based Worldwatch Institute, interviewed Wally and referenced his farming approach in Eat Here, which documents worldwide initiatives in building locally-based food industries.

About the Authors

Roxanne Christensen

Roxanne Christensen co-founded Somerton Tanks Farm, a half-acre demonstration urban farm that served as the U.S. test bed for the SPIN-Farming method from 2003 to 2006. The farm, which was operated in partnership with the Philadelphia Water Department, received the support of the Pennsylvania Dept. Of Agriculture, the Philadelphia Workforce Development Corp., the City Commerce Department, the USDA Natural Resources Conservation Service, the Pennsylvania Department of Environmental Protection, and the Pennsylvania Department of Community and Economic Development.

In 2003, its first year of operation, the farm, located in the sixth largest city in the U.S, produced $26,000 in gross sales from 20,000 square feet of growing space. In 2006 gross sales reached $68,000. In just four years of operation this demonstration farm achieved levels of productivity and financial success that many agricultural professionals claimed were impossible.

Based on the agricultural and financial breakthroughs that were demonstrated at Somerton Tanks Farm, the state of Pennsylvania funded an economic feasibility study that documented the urban farm's economics and projected its maximum income potential to be $120,000 from under an acre of growing space.

As co-author of the SPIN-Farming online learning series, Roxanne's current role is to attract and support new farming talent. She contends that SPIN-Farming is uniquely suited to entrepreneurs and provides a career path for those who have a calling to farm. It is enticing first generation farmers who are keenly interested in matters of principle, but who understand that to have a significant positive impact, they have to function within the existing system, pushing their cause while paying their bills.

"For aspiring farmers, SPIN-Farming eliminates the 2 big barriers to entry – sizeable acreage and substantial startup capital. At the same time, its intensive relay growing techniques and precise revenue targeting formulas push yields to unprecedented levels and result in highly profitable income," Roxanne says. "While most other farming systems focus primarily if not exclusively on agricultural practices, SPIN-Farming emphasizes the business aspects and provides a financial and management framework for having the business drive the agriculture, rather than the other way around."

> "We can't explain GAIA, but we can explain commercial coolers."

As SPIN-Farming becomes established and is practiced more and more widely, Roxanne says, it will create new farmland closer to metropolitan areas, which, in turn will produce environmental, economic and social benefits. "It offers a compelling value proposition."

For more information on SPIN-FARMING please visit *www.spinfarming.com*

Photos courtesy of Somerton Tanks Farm, Philadelphia, PA

The Beginning…

Photo courtesy of Curtis Stone, Green City Acres

Made in the USA
Lexington, KY
29 April 2014